Hasib Sabbagh

From Palestinian Refugee to Citizen of the World

✸

EDITED BY

MARY-JANE DEEB

AND

MARY E. KING

MIDDLE EAST INSTITUTE
UNIVERSITY PRESS OF AMERICA

Copyright © 1996 by
The Middle East Institute

University Press of America, ® Inc.
4720 Boston Way
Lanham, Maryland 20706

3 Henrietta Street
London, WC2E 8LU England

Photograph of Hasib Sabbagh by Richard Ruff,
Green-Wood Photography

British Cataloging in Publication Information Available

Library of Congress Cataloging-in-Publication Data

Hasib Sabbagh : from Palestinian refugee to citizen of the world/
edited by Mary-Jane Deeb and Mary E. King
p.   cm.
l. Sabbagh, Hasib, 1920-. 2. Palestinian Arabs—
Biography. I. Deeb, Mary-Jane. II. King, Mary E.
DS119.7H3776 1996   920'.00929274—20   96-22920 CIP

ISBN 0-916808-43-2 (cloth: alk. paper)
ISBN 0-916808-44-0 (leather: alk. paper)

⊗™The paper used in this publication meets the minimum
requirements of American National Standard for information
Sciences—Permanence of Paper for Printed Library Materials,
ANSI Z39.48–1984

Contents

Preface   v
Mary-Jane Deeb
Mary E. King

Introduction   vii
Jimmy Carter

A Biographical Note   1
Mary-Jane Deeb

Honor All   15
Sana Sabbagh

A Father Like Hasib Sabbagh   19
Suheil H. Sabbagh

Love of Family   21
Robert G. Stone, Jr.

My Friend Hasib   23
Hanna Hourani

A Stateless Statesman   25
Jacob Saliba

A Palestinian Patriot   29
Minos Zombanakis

Hasib   33
Walid Khalidi

There Are Tears in Things 53
Edward W. Said

Adversity Can Be Removed 57
Clovis Maksoud

One Day of Memory 65
Leo J. O'Donovan, S.J.

The Impossible Simply Takes a Little Longer 67
Peter F. Krogh

A Man and His Vision 71
John L. Esposito

A Professional Man 83
George P. Shultz

Be Frank with the World 85
Ray R. Irani

Comfortable with Silence 91
A. Robert Abboud

The Other Refugee 97
Odeh F. Aburdene

A Builder of Hopes 105
David Rockefeller

A Pivotal Role 107
Richard W. Murphy

Preface

The idea for this book originated with Basel Aql, a long-time Palestinian associate and friend of Hasib Sabbagh's in London. It was his view that one can sometimes best grasp the story of a people through the life of a single individual. Having himself experienced a journey similar to Hasib Sabbagh's, he brought the project to life with keen personal interest and the intent to honor his friend on his seventy-fifth birthday. He has prepared a contribution for a companion volume (in Arabic) on Hasib Sabbagh, which will be published in Beirut this year.

Several other people have had a hand in making this publication possible. Richard Murphy of the Council on Foreign Relations, who also chairs the Board of Governors of the Middle East Institute, encouraged this endeavor. MEI president Roscoe Suddarth supported the project enthusiastically and made the book's publication a central part of MEI's fiftieth anniversary celebration. Walid Khalidi of Harvard University gave invaluable advice, for which we are most grateful. Last but not least, we would also like to acknowledge Robin Surratt and Matthew Rieck for preparing the manuscript for publication.

Mary-Jane Deeb
Mary E. King

Hasib Sabbagh with former U.S. president Jimmy Carter, 1986

Introduction

Hasib Sabbagh has for many years been my friend and one of my teachers. He has helped to guide me through both the darkness and the light of the Middle East. As one of the founders of the Carter Center, his interest in our work on conflict resolution has been of inestimable value. Yet what I treasure most is that he has always demonstrated what it means to rise above enmity and bitterness.

In 1948 Hasib Sabbagh lost virtually all his worldly goods. His family home in Safad, near Galilee, was turned into an art gallery—the rooms where his family slept, played, ate, and prayed together converted into an exhibition space. Fleeing, his sister Suad walked on foot for several days to Lebanon. When her shoes wore out, she ripped her headscarf down the middle, tying one half on each foot to cover her bare soles. It was only with the help of the British that Hasib Sabbagh was able to retrieve what little remained of his business in Haifa.

Today, however, it is not of these memories that Hasib Sabbagh speaks. Instead, he remembers the neighboring Jewish firm in Haifa with which he regularly swapped cement when the supply of one or the other ran out. He recalls how, during the 1929 uprisings, his mother put edibles under his hat and beneath the caps of his brothers for them to carry to nearby Jewish families who had suffered in the unrest.

Hasib Sabbagh has dedicated his life to finding a solution to the dilemma of the Palestinian people. His most cherished hope is for the establishment of an independent Palestinian state. It will be as statehood and citizenship become a reality for his people that he will be able to fulfill yet another aspiration: to be able to travel at will, wherever he wants, in the Holy Land. Always looking toward the future rather than the past, he is already making plans to join in the building of a new Middle East—perhaps with a program similar to the Marshall Plan that followed World War II—and he yearns for the development of relationships that will bring prosperity and benefits for all the peoples of the region.

Rosalynn and I have visited with Hasib Sabbagh, his daughter Sana, his sons, and the rest of his family in Athens, London, New York, Washington, and Atlanta. In 1993 we had an unforgettable lunch at his company's installation in Yemen. Flying in for a desert landing at Hodaydah, we gradually made out the Sabbagh camp, at first barely visible. He was waiting there to host us and his staff for the midday meal. Over some of the most difficult terrain I have ever encountered, we watched his teams landing planes, driving trucks, pumping water, servicing oil wells, purifying oil, and pumping it to ships through a new pipeline they had built to the seaport at Makulla. As an engineer by training myself, I could discern how his accomplishment of developing a major oil field in only one year was almost incredible.

Rosalynn and I have seldom had a more interesting and enjoyable experience than our visit to Yemen. We met with the country's top officials, including the president, prime minister, and other government ministers, and I spoke to the newly elected parliament about human rights and democracy. We visited ancient sites in San'a, Aden, Ma'rib, Shibaum, and other places, which until then we had encountered only in the Bible or an encyclopedia. It was a full and rich visit, yet my most vivid memory is still of what I consider the miracle in the desert.

I have found that Hasib Sabbagh lacks two human traits—meanness and pettiness. Treating bigotry and resentment as impostors, he instead welcomes affirmation and magnanimity. He has turned adversity, loss, hurt, and anger into a commitment to reconciliation and peace. From being a man without a country, he has become an exemplar for what it means to be a great citizen of the world.

In the following pages, friends of Hasib Sabbagh's in Europe, the Middle East, and North America recall the varied experiences and incidents they have shared with him. If there be any truth in the contention of the English writer Thomas Carlyle that all history is but biography, then this small volume may also help our understanding of history, for Hasib Sabbagh's life spans most of the twentieth century and teaches us much about one of the world's most vexing conflicts. His story also shows how, ultimately, strife must be overcome in the human heart.

Jimmy Carter

A Biographical Note

Mary-Jane Deeb

When I interviewed Hasib Sabbagh for this essay in late February 1996 at his home in Washington, D.C., I asked him to talk about the factors that had shaped his life and given it its momentum and direction. He listed the major elements, which he believes affect all human beings: namely, their family environment, the people they encounter and associate with, life experiences over which they have no control, and the political environment in which they live. These factors are intricately woven into this biographical essay.

FAMILY LIFE

Hasib Sabbagh was born in 1920 in Tiberias, Palestine. He is a descendant of an old and distinguished family closely related to Ibrahim al-Sabbagh, the personal physician and financial advisor of Dhahir al-'Umar, the Palestinian leader who challenged Ottoman rule in Palestine in the eighteenth century. His grandfather Habib Sabbagh was a deputy of the French consul in Safad, and his uncle Tuma Sabbagh would later become French consul in Safad and Tiberias, as would Tuma's nephew Yusuf upon his uncle's death. Hasib's mother, Faduk, was the eldest child of As'ad al-Khoury, who sought refuge in Safad from the 1860 civil war in Lebanon. As'ad was a self-made man who became a large landowner in the al-Hula region, married into the Haddad family, and had two daughters and five sons.

Mary-Jane Deeb is the editor of the "Middle East Journal" and a professor of international relations at the American University in Washington, D.C.

Hasib's family had a strong influence on his life. His father worked
with the municipal authorities, overseeing the harvest of olives and other
agricultural produce from the nearby villages, assessing their value and
the value of real estate property in the city of Safad, and supervising fishing in Lakes Tiberias and Hula. He taught Hasib the values of hard work
and honesty. The death of his father at the age of fifty-six, when Hasib was
only thirteen, was Hasib's first life-altering experience. His mother Faduk
was left with five daughters and three sons to care for. Although the fourth
in line and the youngest of the three sons, Hasib felt responsible for his
family (and continues to feel that way today). His mother took over the
running of the household, and his aunt—his father's sister—adminis-
tered the family's landholdings. His maternal uncles advised and counseled
the two women, and oversaw the family's interests in the local fisheries.

Faduk Sabbagh was a remarkable woman who, by her example, taught
Hasib to care for others and help those in need. In 1929, for instance, when
the Buraq (Wailing Wall) conflict erupted between Arabs and Jews, and
the Jewish quarter in Safad was burned, Hasib's mother, with her two older
sons, provided daily assistance to the Jewish families of her acquaintance.
She also helped women who had problems with their parents or their
spouses. She allowed them to stay at the Sabbagh home until they had
sorted things out, Faduk often acting as a mediator between the women
and their families. The Sabbagh home was always open to friends, family,
and guests who came for lunch or dinner or even spent the night (because
there were no hotels in Safad at that time). Two Greek Catholic bishops,
Monsignors Hakim and Hajjar, often stayed with the Sabbaghs when they
came to visit their communities in Safad.

In 1948, when Safad was evacuated, Hasib's mother brought together
all her aged relatives and refused to leave her home. The Sabbagh house
soon began to resemble a railway station. Residents of Safad who had fled
to Lebanon earlier, but knew that Faduk alone had remained, began coming back and staying with her; at night they secretly returned to their homes
to collect the belongings they had left behind. When the Jewish authorities
discovered what was going on, they evacuated Faduk to Haifa, and later
moved her and her older relatives to a convent in Nazareth. She remained
in the convent taking care of her relatives until one by one they all died.
She then left in 1953, with the Red Cross, and went to Beirut, where she

Hasib Sabbagh and Diana Tamari on the night of their engagement, 1959

died in 1960. She had lived to attend Hasib's wedding and see her grand-daughter Sana, but did not live to see Hasib's two sons.

It was in 1958, at the age of thirty-eight, that Hasib Sabbagh decided to get married and settle down. He was introduced to many young women in Lebanon, Syria, Jordan, and Egypt but could not find the woman right for him. Then, one day as he was driving down Hamra Street in Beirut, he saw two young women walking who caught his fancy. He followed them until they entered a house. From a nearby drugstore, Hasib called his sister Najla and asked her to join him where he had parked his car. When she arrived he took her to the house where he had seen the two young women enter. Najla recognized the house as that of the Tamari family and agreed to find a way to have Hasib meet the Tamari sisters. The meeting took place in the home of Kamil Deeb, then headmaster of the National Protestant College and also a friend of both the Tamaris and the Sabbaghs.

Hasib and Diana Tamari were engaged a few months later, on New Year's eve 1959, at the Hotel St. George in Beirut. They were married on 8 February of that year by the Greek Catholic bishop George Hakim in a church in Ashrafiya in East Beirut. They took a honeymoon around the world, starting in Europe. They visited Italy, Holland, and England, then they flew to New York, Detroit, Philadelphia, Washington, D.C., San Fran-

Class photograph, Government Arab College, 1938

cisco, and Hawaii. From there they traveled to Asia and visited Japan and India before flying to Kuwait and back to Beirut, where they settled into married life.

They would have three children: Sana, the eldest and the only daughter, was born in December 1959, Suheil in November 1961, and Samir in December 1962. These early years were hard ones because Hasib was in Libya working with the Esso company, often spending days in the desert, where oil had just been discovered. Diana followed Hasib to Libya so that he would not be alone, sometimes leaving the children with her sisters-in-law in Beirut. She traveled with him everywhere he went, including three times around the world. She supported him in his endeavors and understood the demands his work made on his time. She also took care of the children. When they became older, they were sent to school in England. Diana divided her life between her husband and her children, taking care of all, providing support and love as mother, wife, and Hasib's life partner.

On 28 August 1978, Hasib and Diana were in London, where they often spent their summers; they had been invited to dinner that evening. Hasib had left the house earlier for a business meeting, and was planning to return to pick up Diana for dinner when he received a call from his sister Suad saying that Diana was sick. When he arrived home, he discovered that she was unconscious. A doctor was sent for and diagnosed that she had suffered a stroke. She was immediately taken to the hospital, where she died four hours later. This was one of the most devastating experiences Hasib had to face, but he believed it was his duty to go on for the sake of his children, his extended family, and all the people who depended on him.

EDUCATION

Hasib Sabbagh was first sent to a co-educational Catholic school in Safad. Later he and most of his siblings entered public school, while his brother Munir and sister Suad attended private Presbyterian institutions. In school he refused to leave the classroom when it was time for Islamic religious studies, and as a result learned a great deal about Islam. It was also in school that he learned to help those in need: his mother encouraged him to help his weaker classmates with their studies—which he did—and to assist needy students in other ways as well. Hasib also collected money from the better-off students and gave it to the poorest.

As a teenager, Hasib was accepted at the prestigious Government Arab College of Jerusalem, which only the top public school students in Palestine attended. It was headed by Ahmad Samih al-Khalidi and staffed by some of the finest teachers in the Arab world. It was a boarding school with regimental discipline, where the highest standards were set for the students. They were expected to study night and day, and were allowed only one day off for sports and other recreation. It was there that he established some of the friendships that have lasted to this day.

In 1938 Hasib enrolled at the American University of Beirut, as a sophomore, in the college of engineering; attending AUB was to be one of the more significant experiences of his life. Not only was he being trained for his future profession, but he was also exposed to a rich and varied political life. AUB students came from throughout the Arab world, and represented many political currents: there were the Syrian nationalists, followers of Antun Sa'adeh, the communists led by Khalid Bikdash, the Arab nationalists whose ideologue was Professor Constantine Zureik of AUB, and the Arab Ba'thists who adhered to Michel 'Aflaq's ideas.

When World War II broke out, Hasib and his fellow students became politically active, demonstrating against the French and the British, the two main colonial powers in the region. In 1941, AUB students supported Prime Minister Rashid 'Ali al-Kilani's revolt against the British military presence in Iraq. They became so active that the university administration closed AUB, preventing the students from sitting for their end-of-term exams. A compromise was eventually reached whereby the faculty agreed to have the students take their exams orally; Hasib was thus able to graduate that year.

The environment at AUB made Hasib more aware of the problems of the region beyond Palestine and Lebanon. The professors who had the most intellectual influence on Hasib were As'ad Rustum, Constantine Zureik, and Charles Malik, who represented different intellectual schools of thought. AUB was also the place where Hasib would meet more of the people he would be associated with throughout his life, including Salem Khamis from Nazareth, Faraj Bishouty from Safad, Fahmi Karagulla from Iraq, Khalil Ma'luf, Sami Haddad, Farid Haddad, and Raymond Ghosn from Lebanon, Ishaq 'Ali Rida, Wasfi al-Tal, Khalil Salem, and Hamad Farhan from Jordan, Najib Tlil from Jerusalem, and Jawdat Shuhaybar from Gaza.

PROFESSIONAL LIFE

In the summer of 1941, after having graduated from AUB, Hasib returned to Palestine to find a job. The obstacles he encountered led him to make decisions that would change the course of his life. He first attempted to get a job with the public works department in Jerusalem; he met with the British director of the department, who offered him a low-paying job. When Hasib pointed out to him that an unskilled worker in the department made more money, the director responded, "Who says that you know more than a worker at this point?" Hasib rejected the offer and went to Tel Aviv. There, on the advice of his cousin Fawzi Sabbagh, he applied for a job with a Jewish firm that was engaged in work for the British military. The head of the firm did not meet with him, but had him fill out forms and state his salary requirements. Hasib refused to supply a salary requirement and asked that the director inform him of the salary for the position for which he was applying. When the director refused, Hasib put down what he knew others were making in similar jobs. The director then turned down his application on the grounds that he was asking for too much money. These two experiences convinced Hasib that he could not work directly or indirectly for the public sector.

He then considered working for the private sector. On the advice of 'Umar al-Khalil he applied to work as a trainee without pay for an engineering firm headed by Ahmad Faris in Haifa. He slept in the kitchen of the office while learning the ropes. The small business grew, and Faris, along with a new partner, Rushdi al-Imam of Jerusalem, decided to set up their own company and asked Hasib to join them as a full partner. Each man had to put up 500 pounds to start the company. Hasib did not have the money, so he had to borrow it from an uncle. After a year, not only had the company not made a profit, but the original capital had been spent to cover the office expenses of Faris in Haifa and al-Imam in Jerusalem. Realizing that there was little hope that things would improve soon, Hasib decided to leave the firm. When he asked for the return of his investment, he was told that he had no right to anything in the company and would not get his money back. This being Hasib's third negative experience in the workplace, he decided, there and then, that he would never again work for others in the public or private sector.

A lawyer friend, Muhammad Zayid, offered Hasib a room in his office and suggested he go into business for himself. Hasib took his advice and set himself up as a consultant on real estate matters for three lawyers: Muhammad al-Yahya, Subhi al-Khadra, and Ahmad al-Shuqayri (who later became the first leader of the Palestine Liberation Organization [PLO] in 1964). In 1945, when his financial situation improved, Hasib and four other contractors—including Sam'an Qashqush and Muhammad 'Ali Dallul—set up their own engineering office in Haifa, calling it the Consolidated Contractors Company (CCC). Their first contract was to build one hundred apartments for the Haifa municipality for Jewish ex-servicemen from the British army. It was a joint venture with the Arab Building Company, a major construction firm. The building was completed in two years. In 1947, CCC won a contract to build the Iraq Petroleum Company (IPC) headquarters in Haifa, and it was on its way to bigger and better things when the 1948 Arab–Israeli war broke out.

Hasib Sabbagh left Haifa in spring 1948 and went to Beirut, where a number of his brothers and sisters had already sought refuge. He rented a four-bedroom apartment for the entire twenty-five-member family. With a friend, Fahmi Karagulla, he formed a new contracting company, Caracalla, and obtained a construction contract in Iraq in collaboration with IPC. In 1950, he and Karagulla dissolved their partnership, and Hasib set up his own company with his brother-in-law Said Khoury and six other businessmen from Syria and Lebanon, again calling it the Consolidated Contractors Company. It was, at first, headquartered in Hums, Syria, but later moved to Beirut, where Hasib Sabbagh, Said Khoury, and Kamil 'Abd al-Rahman became the sole owners and partners. The company would become one of the largest contracting companies in the Middle East and Hasib Sabbagh's major professional achievement.

In 1950, CCC got a large contract to build pipelines from Kirkuk in Iraq, to Banyas in Syria, and Tripoli in Lebanon. In 1952, CCC was able to obtain a major contract for a Bechtel-Wimpey joint venture, this time in Aden, to build a major refinery and a camp for workers. A year later, CCC took on the building of a major road in Yemen that head of state Imam Ahmad asked him to build. He lived in Aden and traveled regularly to the desert, working sixteen-hour days to ensure that his projects were completed on time. His crew of workers included more than three thousand men, two-thirds of whom were Yemenis, the rest being Palestinians, Lebanese, and Syrians. Hasib was in charge of the financial administration of the business, while Kamil 'Abd al-Rahman took care of the public relations, and Said Khoury supervised the work on the ground.

In 1955, Hasib moved to Saudi Arabia, where he set up a branch of CCC with a new partner, 'Abd al-'Aziz Basim, and an engineer, Michel Nasir. There, in cooperation with major companies such as Bechtel and ARAMCO, CCC began building harbors, water supply systems, hospitals, housing units, highways across the desert, drainage systems, bridges, pipelines, oil refineries, and desalination plants. Hasib's team grew to include Nabil al-Shawa, Fawzi Germanos, Muhammad al-Sa'udi, and a number of others. From Saudi Arabia, Hasib expanded his business to Kuwait in collaboration with 'Abdallah al-Ghanim. They built oil refineries in Ahmadi, and constructed the ports of Mina Sa'ud and Mina 'Abdallah in a Bechtel-Wimpey joint venture, and a camp for the more than two thousand construction workers hired for those projects. CCC also built pipelines and roads, mosques and hospitals, and developed much of Kuwait's infrastructure in the 1950s.

Hasib left Kuwait in 1958, leaving the company in the hands of Said Khoury, and returned to Beirut, where he married Diana the following year. He also opened a new branch of CCC in Amman, Jordan, and put his brother Munir in charge of operations there, assisted by two engineers, Sami Khoury and Birg Klajian. In Jordan, CCC built oil refineries in Zarqa' (with an Italian company, SAIPEM), extended an existing pipeline, and built silos for a phosphates company, as well as roads and an airport. Bechtel then asked CCC to work with the company in Libya, where oil had been found in commercial quantities. In 1961, CCC began building storage facilities for Esso, then pipelines and camps for workers, and refineries for oil companies such as British Petroleum, AGIP, Mobil, Occidental, Hunt, and others. Hasib remained in Libya until 1969, when King Idris was overthrown by Colonel Mu'ammar Qadhdhafi. During those years he expanded CCC's activities to Tunisia and Morocco, and also accepted contracts for projects in the United Arab Emirates, Bahrain, and Qatar. In 1973, CCC set up the National Petroleum Construction Company in Abu Dhabi to provide offshore services to the oil and gas industries in all the countries of the Gulf.

In 1975, when civil war broke out in Lebanon, CCC moved its head-quarters first to London and then to Athens in 1976. Hasib and his family also moved to Athens, while one partner, Said Khoury, continued to live in Kuwait, and the other, Kamil 'Abd al-Rahman, moved to Cannes, France. 'Abd al-Rahman decided in 1976 to sell his share in CCC to Hasib and Said. Three years later, this loyal friend and partner of many years passed away.

In the 1980s, CCC was restructured, and a friend, Fawzi Ka'wash, was made executive vice-president. The CCC partners then attempted to expand the company's operations into Europe, the United States, and Asia. They bought Underwater Engineering, a British firm that worked on un-derwater oil projects, and ACWA, an environmental company; they also bought SICON, an Italian mechanical engineering company specializing in petroleum-related projects. They then acquired a construction firm in the United States, hoping to obtain government contracts for new projects in the United States and abroad. When this did not work out, they sold the company, losing in the process more than three million dollars. They also tried doing business in Pakistan and China, but were unsuccessful.

To diversify its projects, CCC started a partnership with Canadian OXY, and won a bid to explore for oil in Masila, South Yemen. CCC's share was 40 percent. Said Khoury decided that the exploration was too risky and that CCC should sell its share in the project to Shell and American OXY. CCC was left with only a 10 percent share when oil was found in large quantities. Today oil exports from Masila amount to 170,000 barrels per day.

The Iraqi invasion of Kuwait in August 1990 dealt a heavy blow to CCC's operations in the Gulf region. The company had to move all of its employees out of Kuwait and close down its business operations there. With preparations for war and the eventual fighting, all construction projects were halted in Saudi Arabia. In the space of a few months CCC lost thirty million dollars. After the war, the CCC partners undertook new projects in the Arab world. Pipelines were built in Yemen connecting various oil fields to ports on the Red Sea. In Egypt, CCC built roads, sewage systems, and electrical grids, as well as housing for the Egyptian army. CCC also won a bid to rebuild Beirut's international airport. In Mauritania, new roads were built in the desert, and in Kuwait CCC became actively involved in the process of reconstruction. Thus, by the mid-1990s, CCC was thriving once more after having suffered its share of losses and setbacks.

POLITICAL LIFE

Hasib's political life began in the cradle, so to speak. He was born into a family that was involved in politics, although its members never joined any particular political party or group. He grew up in Safad, a city that was representative of the rest of Palestine, where Christians, Muslims, and Jews lived and socialized together. Hasib became aware of the troubles brewing in Palestine between the Arab population, the Jews, and the British in 1929 at the onset of the Buraq conflict. His political education, however, took place at the American University of Beirut, with his exposure to the various political trends represented on campus and the professors there who were the ideologues of some of the most popular of those trends. His political consciousness developed with the Palestinian exodus of 1948 and his new status of refugee in Lebanon. His involvement in the Palestinian cause and his support for those in the diaspora took the form of providing humanitarian assistance to the refugees. Hasib also attended numerous political meetings of Palestinians with different ideas for finding a solution to the Palestinian crisis, but he never became seriously involved with any one group, focusing all his energies on developing his business instead.

In 1970, Hasib met Yasir Arafat, chairman of the PLO, at the house of a mutual friend, Abdul Majid Shoman, in Beirut. Since that time, he has developed a close relationship with Arafat and other members of the PLO leadership. Hasib, Basel Aql, and Walid Khalidi became intermediaries between the PLO and the Lebanese government, trying to inform and explain the complexity of Lebanese confessional politics to Arafat and his colleagues and interceding on behalf of Palestinian refugees with the Lebanese authorities. It was the Lebanese civil war, however, that made Hasib an activist—an activist for peace and reconciliation between the various Lebanese parties and between the Palestinians and the Lebanese.

Hasib recognized the danger of the situation in Lebanon when, in April 1975, twenty-six Palestinians were shot to death by Phalangist forces in

'Ayn al-Rumanah, in retaliation for the assassination of two of their body-guards. The next day, he met with Abu Iyad, the PLO's second in command, at Walid Khalidi's house. The Palestinian leadership had also understood the potential threat to Lebanese–Palestinian relations this incident portended. Abu Iyad asked Hasib to convince the Maronite patriarch, Antonius Butrus Khraysh, to condemn the killing publicly in order to preempt a further deterioration of the situation. Hasib, accompanied by a member of the Phalangist party, visited the patriarch, who agreed to make a statement on the radio that same evening condemning the killings. Hasib also asked the patriarch to invite both Pierre Gemayel, the leader of the Phalangist party, and Yasir Arafat for lunch at the patriarchate to effect a reconciliation between them and their communities. The invitation was accepted by Gemayel, but Arafat declined, saying that it was too soon after the 'Ayn al-Rumanah killings to meet with Gemayel. Hasib Sabbagh strongly believes that had that meeting occurred between the two leaders at the onset of the conflict, it may have prevented much of the bloodshed and disaster that took place in the following days, months, and even years. Hasib was involved in many other efforts to bring leaders of the various factions together in order to resolve conflicts or prevent their escalation.

Throughout the war, Hasib acted as intermediary and mediator, trying to find solutions to the conflict that was destroying the country. He passed messages from the PLO to the U.S. administration and back to the PLO (although he was not the only channel that Arafat used to communicate with the United States). In 1982, after the Israeli invasion of Lebanon, Hasib, accompanied by Munib al-Masri and Abdul Majid Shoman, went to Saudi Arabia to ask King Khalid to intercede with the United States in an effort to stop Israel's bombing of Beirut, to allow the PLO to leave the city. When the bombing stopped, Hasib was instrumental in passing information from the PLO to the United States about the PLO's conditions for its peaceful departure from Beirut.

PHILANTHROPIC ACTIVITIES

Today Hasib Sabbagh is working to promote the peace process in Gaza and the West Bank. He is a member of the Palestine National Council as well as a member of the Palestine Central Council, where he has played an important role over the years. He is also deputy chairman of the Health Care Organization of the West Bank and Gaza and chairman of the Palestinian Students Fund, which provide social and economic services to residents of the West Bank and Gaza. To promote the training and education of young Palestinian men and women, he gives financial aid on an annual basis to educational institutions such as al-Najah University in Nablus, Bethlehem University, the Islamic University in Gaza, the Gaza National College, and Bir Zeit University in the West Bank.

Hasib has not limited his assistance to Palestinians, but has also given generously to other causes. After the death of his wife, he founded the Diana Tamari Sabbagh Foundation, which receives 1 percent of his annual income and distributes it to a wide variety of institutions in the Middle East, Europe, and the United States. He has given financial aid to the Beirut Charities Foundation, the American University of Beirut, the Jordan Charities Foundation, the Welfare Association in Geneva, and the Vatican. In the United States he has been generous to health care and educational institutions primarily. The Cleveland Clinic Foundation and the Massachusetts General Hospital in Boston have received generous grants from the Diana Tamari Sabbagh Foundation, as has Harvard University (the alma mater of his daughter Sana), Georgetown University (in particular the Center for Muslim–Christian Understanding), the American Enterprise Institute, a Washington, D.C., think tank, Eureka College in California, and Webber College in Florida (where his sons studied). In 1995, he made a generous donation to the Council on Foreign Relations in New York to create a chair in Middle East affairs. It is now occupied by Richard Murphy, a former assistant secretary of state for Near Eastern and South Asian affairs (1983–89) and the present chairman of the Board of Governors of the Middle East Institute in Washington, D.C.

Hasib Sabbagh, Queen Noor of Jordan, and Sana Sabbagh

Honor All

Sana Sabbagh

Only a week after my mother died, a family member approached me and asked me not to go to the United States for college, but rather to stay and take care of my father. I was already in a state of dismay and profoundly grief-stricken over my mother's sudden and premature death at the age of forty-six, and now here was an admonition that baffled and confused me. I felt as if my mother had left me, abandoned me—disappeared. In the months preceding my mother's death, she and I had become increasingly worried about my father's health. With her death, he, too, was now devastated. Until then, my father had been to me a powerful giant, calm and serene. My world was shaken as I watched him cry for the first time in my sixteen years. The two months immediately following my mother's death were a haze of receiving lines, greetings and handshakes, and faces I had never before encountered. As the days passed, more and more of my relatives suggested that I forego my American dream and stay with my father, shuttling between London and Athens.

I had been trying for some time to gain admittance to Harvard University, and I had finally succeeded. My father knew how much this acceptance meant to me. One evening while we were alone, I sat next to my father and asked him whether he wanted me to cancel my plans and stay with him. I had already made the decision that I would stay if this was what he wanted. He looked at me in the most tender way and said calmly but clearly, "No, you should go." My heart was trembling. My father—so loving, selfless, and stoic—needed me, and I knew it. Yet he was ready to sacrifice his

Sana Sabbagh is the daughter of Hasib and Diana Sabbagh.

needs for my future. I was so grateful; the bond between us grew even stronger. In short order, I left for Cambridge, but ever since that moment I have consciously made my father the first priority in my life; he always comes first for me, because he put me first. During my first year at Harvard, we spoke to each other everyday by telephone, no matter where in the world he was. Since then, I have spent every vacation or long weekend with him.

My father's purity of heart is one of the strongest and most powerful forces in my life. He is motivated by the merit of a cause rather than by the prestige that he might derive from helping it. Uncannily, he is able to detach himself and submerge whatever self-interest he may have in order to get a job done or to make necessary decisions. One of his most remarkable traits is that he always allows others—his friends or collaborators, whether in business or philanthropy—to take the credit while he quietly leads and steers them. He is the most unassuming, yet powerful and insightful leader I have encountered. Once he has committed himself to a quest, he is unrelenting.

When our family was living in Beirut, four different illustrated and framed copies of a Rudyard Kipling poem hung on the walls of various parts of our home. My father taught me how to read the poem in English at the age of ten (before I was fluent in the language). He urged me to adopt Kipling's words as my motto, just as he had made them his:

> If you can keep your head when all about you
>   Are losing theirs and blaming it on you;
> If you can trust yourself when all men doubt you,
>   But make allowance for their doubting too,
> If you can wait and not be tired by waiting,
>   Or, being lied about, don't deal in lies,
> Or being hated, don't give way to hating,
>   And yet don't look too good, nor talk too wise; . . .
>
> If you can meet with Triumph and Disaster
>   And treat those two impostors just the same: . . .
> Or watch the things you gave your life to, broken,
>   And stoop and build 'em up with worn-out tools . . .

If you can force your heart and nerve and sinew
    To serve your turn long after they are gone,
And so hold on when there is nothing in you
    Except the Will which says to them: "Hold on!"

If you can talk with crowds and keep your virtue,
    Or walk with Kings—nor lose the common touch,
If neither foes nor loving friends can hurt you,
    If all men count with you, but none too much . . .
Yours is the Earth and everything that's in it . . .

As I was growing up, I used to wonder how my father had achieved such self-possession; how did he develop the quiet spirit of repose that is at his core? Years after I was fully grown, I came upon some lines from Pope John XXIII that spoke to me and seemed almost perfectly to describe the creed that has led to my father's understanding and wisdom:

Hear all; believe a few; honor all.
Do not believe everything you hear;
Do not judge everything you see;
Do not do everything you can;
Do not give everything you have;
Do not say everything you know;
Pray, read, withdraw, be silent, be at peace.

My father's generosity is boundless; he is the most altruistic individual I have ever met or known. He has given me unending and unreserved acceptance. If I have ever disappointed him, he has not allowed it to affect our relationship, his confidence in me, or his depth of caring. I owe him everything and love him unconditionally.

Recently, my father met with a group of U.S. senators over lunch on Capitol Hill. The topic of discussion was the peace process in the Middle East. After my father had given his views, one of the senators stood up and posed the question, "What can we do for you personally, sir?" "An identity," my father replied. "I need an identity. I have fulfilled all my dreams and ambitions except one. I do not have an identity if I die. As a Palestinian, I want to be buried in Safad, in Galilee."

When my father had finished, I realized that he was preparing for his death. Instead, I urged him to continue planning. Armand Hammer, whom we knew, had been making ten- and twenty-year plans after he had turned ninety years of age. "Make a twenty-year plan," I pleaded with my father. I promised him that I would, to the best of my ability, take him—may God delay the day—to rest in Safad.

Father, I need you. Suheil and Samir need you. CCC needs you. The Arab world needs you. Palestine needs you.

A Father Like Hasib Sabbagh

Suheil H. Sabbagh

Having a father like Hasib has been both an honor and a challenge. I have learned so much from him—from the stories he told me, and the advice he gave me. He has an answer for everything. His generosity is amazing; his office is open to everybody, executive or clerk alike. He is always willing to assist people in times of need.

If there is one thing I have learned from my father, it is never to give up. He has traveled to the ends of the world to help me find a solution to my stuttering. He has always advised me to think positively to achieve my goals. I am deeply grateful to my father for helping me conquer one of the most difficult obstacles that I have had to face in my life.

It certainly is a challenge to attempt to fill the shoes of such a man. Pleasing him has always been my top priority, even though at times I have felt I disappointed him. Regardless, he has always been there to guide me. I can only wish to be as good a father to my children as he has always been to me.

Suheil H. Sabbagh is the son of Hasib and Diana Sabbagh.

Hasib Sabbagh and his family sitting for a portrait in 1962: (left to right) Samir, Sana, Diana, and Suheil

Love of Family

Robert G. Stone, Jr.

It was at his daughter Sana's graduation from Harvard, in the spring of 1982, that I first met Hasib Sabbagh. We were introduced by a mutual friend, Professor A. J. Meyer, who was active in the Middle East center there. The sparkle in Hasib's eyes on that occasion bespoke his pride in and love for Sana, both of which have only intensified over the intervening years.

During that summer, three of us were beneficiaries of Hasib's hospitality in Athens: Professor Meyer, Professor Ned Keenan, who was then director of Harvard's Middle East center, and me. We met many members of Hasib's large family, and had a glorious day on his yacht visiting one of the Greek isles. It was there, at a charming waterfront restaurant, that Hasib's love for the sea and fishing revealed itself. We watched in awe as he ordered six or seven courses of fish, each prepared to his own specifications.

Subsequently, I made other trips to Greece, once being included in a Sabbagh family celebration where uncles, aunts, and cousins by the dozens took over the largest part of a Greek restaurant with much dancing and great fun. Again, Hasib's love of family manifested itself. He was so happy, caring,and genuinely devoted to them all.

My admiration for Hasib stems from our many conversations and discussions about life in general and, most particularly, about the politics of the Middle East, an area about which he is eminently knowledgeable and practical (and frustrated at times)—so sound in his thinking that his advice

---

Robert G. Stone, Jr., is chairman of the board of Harvard University.

has been sought by persons in all walks of life, both in the United States and abroad.

I wish to express my particular thanks to Hasib for his advice and assistance to Harvard University and to its Middle East center and related studies. His foresight and guidance have been of inestimable value.

My Friend Hasib

Hanna Hourani

Hasib and I became friends in 1939. He graduated from the American University of Beirut (AUB) with a degree in engineering in 1941, the year I entered AUB as a freshman. As a student, he was serious but also loved his fun. He was our "godfather," so to speak, and my father appointed him as my guardian and paid him pocket money. I have known Hasib as a sincere friend. He is loving, warm, and a great giver. These traits he inherited from his mother, God bless her soul. Here I shall say only a few personal things.

On one occasion while I was forbidden to leave the campus of AUB as punishment for a wrong I had done, Hasib and some friends were having a party that evening and the party could not be complete without me. As a result, Hasib came up with the plan to hire a taxi and get me off campus in the trunk of the car. I arrived without incident at the party. The return journey was different, however. When we got to the gate of AUB, the guard refused to allow Hasib to go inside with the car, because it was late. They argued for some time; meanwhile, I could not breathe in the trunk. I started yelling, so Hasib ordered the driver to speed away. We then drove around to one of the walls of AUB, where I climbed on the shoulders of Hasib and jumped over the walls and onto campus.

The story of our life together is one full of love and tears. Way back in the 1960s, Hasib, his wife Diana, my wife Laila, and I went for a drive outside London. I was driving. A fast-moving car nearly hit us, and my wife could have been killed; luckily we escaped. Diana then asked me what

Hanna Hourani is a lawyer and long-time friend of Hasib Sabbagh.

T. Al Ghosein, Hasib Sabbagh, Basel Aql, Said Khoury, and Hanna Hourani in Cobham, England, 1995

I would have done had Laila died. I said it would have meant the end of me. Diana then turned to Hasib and asked him the same question. Hasib, according to Diana, gave the wrong answer when he said he would have had to go on living to bring up the children. A nice argument ensued. The irony of life came into play later: Hasib lost his Diana in 1978, and I lost my Laila in 1980. Hasib and I then entered into a phase of our lives shrouded in sadness.

On a happier note, in 1966 the four of us had gone for a holiday in Europe. While in Prague, we bought Czech money for our expenses. On our day of departure we realized that we had more money than we needed. We had no idea what to do with the extra money, as we were not allowed to take it out of the country. Hasib whispered in my ear to put the money in Laila's bag. Foolishly I did, and we were lucky enough to escape a search. Once we were out of potential trouble we had a good laugh about what we had done.

May God grant Hasib health and happiness.

A Stateless Statesman

Jacob Saliba

> Lives of great men all remind us
> We can make our lives sublime,
> And departing, leave behind us
> Footprints on the sands of time.
>
> —*Henry Wadsworth Longfellow*

Hasib Sabbagh has fulfilled Longfellow's poetic reminder with character, dedication, and generosity and, best of all, with love for his fellow human beings. This has earned him the respect and trust of peasants and royalty alike. Yet, Hasib is one of the most humble persons that I have ever known. In the last seventy-five highly productive years of his life, Hasib Sabbagh has again and again shown himself to be equally comfortable with laborers and kings. He has never lost the commonplace touch that is the hallmark of true greatness.

A man of few words but deep thoughts, he has positively affected the lives of hundreds of individuals; I will always remember one of my earliest meetings with Hasib and his wife Diana. We were enjoying lunch by the harbor in Athens, and Diana and I were actively engaged in animated conversation. Hasib was listening. Diana complained to me that Hasib was endangering his life by spending too much time on what was then apparently considered a hopeless cause. Hasib's short reply was, "If I do not do it, then who will?" This is his creed and philosophy.

Jacob Saliba is a businessman and industrialist.

Hasib's generosity is not limited to personal resources. He also gives of himself, deeply, including perhaps the most precious commodity of all—time. He has probably been the largest single donor to Palestinian causes. His philanthropic endeavors have been international in scope and have involved institutions such as hospitals, educational foundations, orphanages, and many other charities. Hasib believes in both physically and financially backing causes and programs that appeal to his sense of social and humanitarian responsibility. Let me cite but one example.

Because of his many interests in the Boston area, partly centered around Harvard University, and due to my involvement at Massachusetts General Hospital, when Hasib needed an expert medical opinion it was natural for me to introduce Hasib to Dr. Roman DeSanctis, the hospital's chief of clinical cardiology. An immediate friendship developed between Hasib and Dr. DeSanctis, and, in return for Dr. DeSanctis' care and friendship, Hasib has made contributions to the Massachusetts General Hospital, one of the many such institutions that has benefited from his generosity. Having been associated with Hasib in some of his American philanthropic activities, I have observed, time and again, how diligently he tries to avoid the lime-light of publicity and does not give gifts in order to gain prestige, improve his image, or seek notoriety. Quite the opposite, he draws no attention to himself.

Hasib's schedule of appointments would exhaust a person half his age, yet he has never been too busy to lend a caring hand to a friend and, at times, to a friend of a friend. Because of my medical associations, I have received many overseas calls from Hasib requesting my help in arranging admissions for friends, and often his pleas were for persons who were strangers to him, but whose problems had touched his heart.

In spite of his many achievements, a great sadness has filled Hasib's life. He and the entire Sabbagh family have been stateless for almost fifty years. I say this being mindful of the possibility that only one who is without a country can fully understand the dimensions of this tragic situation. A residence is not a home: one can only have a home if one has a country, so to be without a country is to be homeless, even if one can afford beautiful residences in many countries. Even though Hasib could qualify for citizenship in many of the countries where he actually owns houses, he is a Palestinian—and, to him, Palestine is his homeland. He yearns for the

The Sabbagh family home in Safad

day when he can return there and reclaim his nationality as a Palestinian. Although Hasib's magnificent residences in the Middle East, Europe, and in the United States have always been readily connected by his personal jets and the Concorde, I have the feeling that the simple time-tested lines of John Howard Payne may reflect Hasib Sabbagh's true feelings.

> Mid pleasures and palaces though we may roam,
> Be it ever so humble,
> There is no place like home.

It may be difficult for one who has not experienced the dislocation suffered by the Sabbagh family to comprehend, but I believe that Hasib would probably rather live in a lean-to or shed in Palestine than to have five mansions in the heart of Paris or Rome. Recently Hasib confided to me that both his wife Diana and his sister Suad had wished to be buried in

Palestine, and that his own inability to fulfill their last wishes pained him profoundly.

I amuse myself in thinking that Hasib and I are both charter members of the Open-Heart Bypass Club. After my first major surgical operation in 1979, at Massachusetts General Hospital, one of the first persons to visit me in my room was Hasib, who had flown in from London. Some ten years later, I would be at his bedside at the Cleveland Clinic. Then on December 2, 1994, once again, I had to undergo the same operation, and this time Hasib was in London. Through mutual friends, he discovered that I was back in the hospital. His visit to me a few days later was more comforting and soothing than any balm.

I know of no one who is more active than the businessman and statesman Hasib Sabbagh. Hasib Sabbagh's contacts are worldwide and extend into all social strata. Because of his involvement with the Palestinian cause, he has for years been conversing with leading heads of state and political leaders. Yet, he is equally comfortable with Bedouins and rural folk who respect his honesty and devotion to his cause. I also know of no one who has a higher standard when it comes to personal loyalty to his friends. Hasib's visit to my bedside in December 1994 meant the rearrangement of already hectic schedules involving numbers of engineers, staff, and host-country officials. It was accomplished at considerable personal inconvenience, yet this stateless statesman insisted on changing his plans in order to support a friend.

A Palestinian Patriot

Minos Zombanakis

It is curious how people from different parts of the world and from different backgrounds meet and subsequently become "friends for life." This is the case with Hasib Sabbagh and myself. He is Palestinian, and I am Greek. In Saudi Arabia, in the mid-1970s, I first met Hasib Sabbagh. He was there with some of his colleagues in connection with a business trip; we were at the home of a mutual friend when Hasib told me that he had an important appointment with the minister of planning. "Is it about your company," I asked. "Not at all," Hasib responded. It was to try to impress upon the Saudi minister of government the need to employ the services of a technical consultancy group that was based in Lebanon and composed exclusively of young graduate Palestinians. Hasib was sacrificing a crucial opportunity for his own firm in order to plead the case of a group of Palestinian refugees who were just starting out in life. This is how I became aware of Hasib's strength of character and his keen interest in his fellow Palestinians—an interest that has grown stronger with the years. We have been meeting regularly with each other ever since our meeting in the 1970s.

Hasib is, by nature, a deeply moral person, positive in his thinking and outlook, and these are the qualities that must have helped him so often to overcome the many hardships he has encountered throughout his life. I think these attributes are also responsible for his many successes. He trusts people, and there are those who have sometimes tried to take advantage of

Minos Zombanakis is a finance advisor and consultant.

his good nature; yet, he prefers to remain trusting. I think it is a conscious decision on his part not to harden himself or throw up fragile defenses. Hasib's optimism knows no boundaries. I remember conversations with him during devastating events, such as the destruction of Lebanon, and at excruciatingly painful times, such as when he lost his beloved wife Diana, the center of his life. Remarkably he was able to find comforting words at such moments to console himself and his guests.

A deep thinker and a proud man—proud of what he is and of what he has achieved in life—he has remained a person of exceptional humility and is always seeking opportunities to help others. His generosity is by now legendary, yet you will never find out from him what he gives away. He believes in the ethic that "one's left hand should not know what the right hand gives."

Our relationship has, for the past twenty years, been based on a most personal affinity. We have never done any business together. Hasib puts the person first and foremost; business may or may not follow. I always found being in his company to be appealing because he is vitally interested in people and world events. I appreciate the sincerity and clarity of his thinking and his common sense. You are never in doubt that he is a Palestinian patriot, but that fact never prevents him from judging others with objectivity and evenhandedness, nor has his fundamental integrity restrained him from criticizing his own people or praising their enemies when merited. Hasib avoids fanaticism. He has no use for excessive zeal or extremism of any sort. For example, though he is a Christian, he has been pressing the Greek government to build a mosque in Athens.

It was after he became concerned about the ability of his employees to continue to work with safety in and from Lebanon that Hasib began to think about settling in Greece; in due time, he made the decision to shift the center of his operations to Athens. He has been a credit to our country for almost two decades, both directly through large remittances to cover the expenses of his operation, and indirectly by settling a number of excellent people from the Middle East in our country. His company grew substantially, and he constructed a building for his own offices. I can boldly say that we Greeks are filled with admiration for him and his family. In one other way, he sets an important standard: No separation exists between his private self and his public personage; he is always the same

Suad, Sana, Hasib, and Diana Sabbagh at the
Church of the Holy Sepulcher, 1961

unaffected, down-to-earth person. He does not put on a public face. There is no mask.

Hasib's late wife Diana meant more to him than mere words can convey, and I personally do not think that he has every recovered from her loss. After her death he focused his attention on his children, with the help of his cherished sister Suad, who shared and managed his homes until her recent death. Anyone who was privileged enough to be allowed into the heart of the family could see how he respected and cared for his sister. I always found myself strangely comforted about the human race when witnessing his tenderness toward her, and his family environment in general.

Hasib is, along with his brother-in-law and partner Said Khoury, the largest contractor in the Middle East. He knows heads of governments, kings, and princes. He can telephone virtually any corporate board room. He commands respect from all who know him, yet, when all is said and done, Hasib remains a man devoted to the simple, tested values and verities of life, and he is committed to the highest principles. One cannot help but say, "I am glad that life's path has brought me to know Hasib."

I wish him a happy birthday and many happy returns.

Basel Aql, Hasib Sabbagh, PLO chairman Yasir Arafat, and Walid Khalidi in Beirut, 1978

Hasib

Walid Khalidi

I met Hasib Sabbagh for the first time in 1972 in Beirut, but his name
had been familiar to me since the late 1930s, when he was a pupil at the
Government Arab College in Jerusalem, whose principal was my father,
the principal's residence being just behind the main college building. The
fact that Hasib was a pupil at the Arab College already says a lot about
him. The college was the apex of the Arab, male public (in the American
sense) educational system. (The Jewish counterpart of this system was
autonomous, under the aegis of the elected Jewish general council, the
Vaad Leumi.)

The philosophy underlying the college's purpose and curriculum was
élitist in the best sense of the word. Admission to it was based exclusively
on merit and the most stringent entrance qualifications. Although a boarding institution, its fees were nominal. Entrants were at the top of their
classes at the mid-high school level, where the college classes began. Its
recruitment network encompassed the entire country, generating the stiff-
est competition among applicants and tapping the best Arab talent
irrespective of social or financial status. The total number of students in
any one year never exceeded one hundred. The faculty, graduates of the
best British universities, were mostly Arab. The curriculum was a bal-
anced synthesis of the humanities and the sciences as well as of Arab Islamic
culture and the Western classical heritage, both Greek and Latin being
taught. Originally conceived as a teacher's training college, it evolved into

*Walid Khalidi is Research Fellow at the Center for Middle Eastern Studies at
Harvard University in Cambridge, Massachusetts.*

a university college affiliated with the University of London. Through what were then known as the matriculation and intermediate examinations—the equivalents of the modern British O and A levels, respectively—the pupils moved to an external bachelor's degree from the University of London. Had Palestine not fallen in 1948, the college would have become its national university. In most ways, the Arab College was unique in the Arab world, and possibly in the Third World. Its graduates constitute to this day an elite with their own *esprit de corps.*

Between the 1930s and the time our very different paths finally converged in 1972, the watershed year in Hasib's life and mine—as for all Palestinians—was, of course, 1948. The events of that year have remained a permanent item on our agenda as, day after day and over the years, Hasib and I "tired the sun with talking and sent it down the sky." Coaxing his memory, the following is what I have pieced from Hasib's account of how he left Haifa, his adopted city, and second only, in his eyes, to what was for him the true capital of Palestine, his hometown Safad.

Hasib's Tale

When the final Jewish onslaught came on 23 April, Arab morale broke down and there started a panicky flight from the city by land and sea. The British forces escorted convoy after convoy out of town, facilitating the evacuation of Haifa. We lived in the Abbas quarter, and close by was the house of George Mu'ammar, a business partner and an active member of Haifa's National Committee. Mu'ammar was very upset by the flight of Haifa's residents, and I can still see him standing on his balcony, haranguing the crowds surging by below, pleading with them not to leave. When I saw this I ran up to him and shouted: "What on earth are you doing? Leave these people alone! Can't you see that if they stay and get killed, you will be blamed?" He persisted, but I pulled him down and made him stop.

I myself had decided to go to Safad, my hometown, which was in the middle of Arab territory and strongly held by us. But with the fighting in eastern and western Galilee at the time, the easiest way to reach Safad was from the north, through south Lebanon, which meant I had first to go to Beirut. Our company had lorries in Haifa, and I invited anybody who wanted to travel to Beirut to climb on board. Soon the lorries were crammed to capacity, and the British escorted us to the Lebanese frontier. We arrived in Beirut on the afternoon of 23 April. There I met Captain Emile Jumay'an, who was with the Transjordanian Arab Legion and an old family friend. I told him I had just come from Haifa, which had fallen, and he asked me what I intended to do. I said I was going to Safad after seeing my brother Habib and my sister Suad, who had just come from there. He told me not to go, although he was on his way there himself on a mission involving the garrison under the command of the Arab League's military committee based in Damascus. When my brother Habib, who had been sent by the Safad National Committee to get arms and ammunition, heard what Jumay'an had to say, he decided to stay behind in Beirut. But my sister Suad, who had come to Beirut on behalf of the Red Crescent to take back medicines and bandages, insisted on completing her mission regardless.

After two weeks in Beirut, I set off for Safad myself. But when I reached the border on 9 May, masses of people were coming from the direction of Safad, among them my brother Munir and my sister Suad, who was disheveled, barefooted, and with torn clothing. Safad had fallen, so we returned to Beirut, and, as I contemplated our situation, I decided that what the family most urgently needed was money. We had plenty in Barclays Bank in Haifa, so I made up my mind to return there, and set off by sea from Tyre. The journey was stormy and the boat was packed, with everybody vomiting over everybody else. The boat docked in the harbor near the government hospital on 10 May, five days before the end of the British Mandate. Arriving in the city we saw both British and Haganah forces. The Haganah troops looked at our identity cards and, the mandate still being in force, allowed us in. I made my way to our house in Abbas. Shops were closed, the streets were empty, and Haganah troops were all over. Our house had not been touched. Soon after my arrival, I went to call on Mu'ammar, who was delighted to see me. He chided me for leaving, and tried to convince me to stay: "If you stay behind, you and I can do a lot of business together." I said I had come only to withdraw money from the bank.

The next day I went to Barclays, which was open, and withdrew 20,000 pounds in cash. On the way home, I dropped by the Municipality, where I was greeted in a friendly way by my Jewish friends who were at their posts. They urged me to stay in town, joking that they needed me for protection against the Arab armies. I said I had come to collect money to help my family, given their situation since the fall of Safad, and had to return to Beirut. From the Municipality I went to Mu'ammar's house to bid him farewell. Again, he urged me to stay, but when I refused he asked me to take his wife and daughter with me to Beirut, which I did. The daughter was seventeen years of age at the time and had been unhinged by what she had just gone through; to this day she is in a mental hospital, where I have been taking care of her all these years. Mu'ammar himself was a rather stingy person. He was not harmed by the Jews, but some years later he was stabbed in the stomach by his cook during an altercation and died.

I left Haifa for the last time on 14 May. When we got into Beirut harbor on 15 May, security people came on board and said that all the women and children could disembark in Beirut, but that the men had to return to where they had come from. It was a government order that had to be obeyed without exception. I immediately started trying to contact my Lebanese friends and, in no time, had reached Hamid Frangieh, who was foreign minister at the time. Frangieh wrote a letter to the security forces on official stationery, which was presented to the security people at the harbor, instructing them to allow all the passengers on that particular ship to disembark. So, because of me, scores of other males were able to go ashore in Beirut on 15 May.

One may not agree with some aspects of Hasib's conduct in Haifa on that fateful day of 23 April 1948, such as his chiding of George Mu'ammar for urging people to stay. Yet even a cursory look at this account would at once reveal Hasib's timber—the attributes that had already stood him in good stead and still do to this day: self-confidence, courage, decisiveness, dynamism, resourcefulness, perseverance, and commitment to those for whom he feels responsible. It also reveals how, early in his career, he had begun establishing the wide range of friends he enjoys today—from Jewish municipal officials in Haifa to an officer in the Transjordanian Arab Legion to the foreign minister of Lebanon. Most telling of all, however, it reveals the transparency of his *bona fides*: Even though he had (not uncharacteristically) literally "tackled" George Mu'ammar, the two remained close friends.

In addition to the light it throws on the circumstances of Hasib's own departure from Palestine, his account is also of general historical interest. Among other things, it shows that contrary to Zionist claims, the Arab authorities—whether Palestinian (Mu'ammar, as a member of the National Committee of Haifa) or Lebanese (the security authorities at the Beirut port)—were opposed to the exodus of Palestinians from their country.

It was in the idyllic pre-civil war days of Lebanon that Hasib and I first met over a lunch arranged by a mutual friend. We discovered that we shared certain sentiments: a searing conviction about the monumental injustice inflicted on the Palestinian people and a compelling urge to alleviate their plight, both coupled with a belief in the common destiny of all Arab countries and the imperative for these countries to coordinate with each other, if only to remain on the map of the fast-changing modern world.

To many Arabs, but particularly to the Palestinian "generation of 1948," to which both Hasib and I belong, the 1967 war and its catastrophic consequences—the occupation of the rump of Palestine in the West Bank, including East Jerusalem and the Gaza Strip, as well as of the whole of Sinai and the Golan—had been like a dagger twisted in a festering wound. Soon after the war, some friends and I at the American University of Beirut—notably, the economist Burhan Dajani and the physicist Antoine Zahlan—met for a succession of postmortems. We all agreed that the Israeli victory of 1967, as in 1948, was a result of a deep malaise in Arab society, at the heart of which was the stifling of the Arab individual by the various Arab regimes. The most costly result of this was the alienation of the best Arab talent and their exodus to the West.

We thought that one way to address this issue would be to establish a nonprofit institute or center somewhere in the Arab world that could lure back the best brains that had emigrated, making it the meeting ground for interaction between them and those who had stayed. With luck the center would become a model for others. Such a center would need a library, research equipment, physical facilities, material incentives for its staff, the necessary financial resources, and, of course, a research program focused on societal priorities. Thus the operational questions boiled down to which Arab country was to be the site of the center, where the funds were to be obtained, how to ensure the benign sponsorship of the host government, and what focus to choose for our activities.

Clearly the most hospitable country would have been Lebanon, because of its open political environment and lifestyle. The distinguished historian Constantine Zureik and I—together with Dajani, Isam Ashour (a wizard at financial management), and others—had already, in 1963, founded the inter-Arab Institute for Palestine Studies in Beirut as a Lebanese corporation. But our commitments to IPS compounded our difficulties in securing the necessary funds for the proposed new center. How could we meet our responsibility to IPS and ensure additional funds for another institution? Despite our strong preference for an independent private center unaffiliated with any government, as was the case with IPS, the search for adequate funding obliged us to consider governmental financial support.

After weighing the alternatives, we decided to seek the funds and sponsorship directly from King Hussein in Amman. Our focus would be the technological gap between the Arab countries and the West. We were not to be disappointed. A meeting with the king, in late 1967, which included Dajani, Zahlan, and myself, elicited within one hour a truly regal response and commitment. Within months, the Royal Scientific Society (RSS) was established with funds provided by the king. A board of trustees under the chairmanship of Crown Prince Hasan included the three of us from Beirut, as well as Abdul Salam al-Majali (the current prime minister of Jordan) and the late, much lamented former prime minister Abdul Hamid Sharaf, a former student of mine. Zahlan resigned from his AUB physics chair to become director of RSS and a galaxy of two score hand-picked experts from the diaspora and the Arab countries went briskly to work in what seemed to be unimaginably ideal conditions; stern reality soon intervened, however. The 1970 confrontation between the Palestine Liberation Organization (PLO) and the Jordanian government was upon us. This necessitated our disengagement and return to our "bases" in Beirut. The RSS is still thriving—an almost solitary beacon in the research deserts of the Arab world.

With Amman out of the picture, our next choice as host country was Egypt. President Gamal Abdul Nasser had, in the meantime, died, exhausted by his efforts to end the fighting in Jordan. By now we had been joined by the Palestinian businessman Ramzi Dalloul. Our main contact in Cairo was Muhammad Hasanein Haikal, Nasser's confidant and an old friend. Haikal was attentive as we explained our purpose. "Why didn't you come to us first?" he asked. We couldn't say we had preferred Amman. He finally said that some oil-rich Arab countries had expressed the desire to commemorate the late president and that there was talk of erecting a massive monument for him. Our project had come just in time, he said, and would be a more worthy alternative. He would immediately set to work to get the necessary endorsement, and we should return to hear the good news in a few weeks' time. We were thrilled, but when we did return, there was a palpable change in Haikal's attitude. The situation was not as easy as he had at first thought, he stated. As he struggled with his explanation, it was plain to us that our project's chances in Egypt had met their demise.

It was not long after I had met Hasib that we broached the idea of the center to him. As the architect and driving force of the largest, most successful and efficient private Arab corporation of its kind, he immediately understood the significance of the center. After listening intently, he firmly made up his mind. He would back the endeavor all the way; the project had met its ideal sponsor. The new corporation would be named Arab Projects and Development (APD) and be headquartered in Lebanon. It would be nonprofit in the sense that all net income—after meeting the operational expenses and handsomely remunerating its professional staff—would be plowed back into it for continuous improvement and expansion. The basic idea behind APD was the same as that behind RSS, except that APD was completely private and revenue-earning, although not profit-seeking. APD's board of trustees included Hasib, Dajani, Zahlan, myself, and Dalloul, who was named as chairman; Zahlan was appointed director. The talent that had dispersed after our disengagement from Amman was reassembled and expanded, and we set to work with renewed vigor and enthusiasm. APD landed several major contracts in the rapidly expanding economy of Iraq, one of its first being to undertake a systematic, scientific country-wide survey of high-level manpower in Iraq, the first of its kind anywhere in the Arab world. This study became the basis for the sweeping modernization of the country that followed.

Hasib was "Mr. Can-Do" personified. Action for him was the art of making the impossible possible. Where I weighed the pros and cons, he simply forged ahead, undeterred by the possibility of failure. Yet, his seeming impetuosity hid a shrewd intuition and an uncanny sense for opportunity. Thus a complementarity evolved in our partnership, which was as dynamic as it was exhilarating, without precluding moments of mutual irritation.

The only other Arab person I have known comparable to Hasib in terms of his action orientation, boundless energy, and public spiritedness was the late Lebanese Maronite entrepreneur Emile Boustani. Hasib was an admirer of Emile, and I believe that he derived his inspiration, at least partly, from him. Boustani had been a pioneer in the contracting business in the Arab world outside Egypt. He had started his Contracting and Trading Company (CAT) in the early 1940s in Haifa, where the two had met. A basic difference existed between the two in motivation, however; whereas Hasib was a stranger to political ambition, Emile aimed at the highest political office in Lebanon—the presidency. Indeed, if any one individual could have saved Lebanon from the horrors of its civil war, it would have been Boustani as president. But this was not to be. On 15 March 1963, Boustani, accompanied by his inseparable friend, the brilliantly iconoclastic Palestinian bacteriologist Nimr Tuqan, tragically died when his private plane crashed into the Bay of Jounieh off Beirut.

One small incident, which took place during the Tripartite invasion of Egypt, captures the spirit of Boustani. I was a university lecturer at Oxford at the time, and had gone to London to visit the Egyptian embassy; afterwards I was to meet Emile for dinner, who had earlier won the confidence of Nasser and was on some sort of mediating mission. As I was walking out of the embassy, I noticed a young man in his late teens sobbing quietly in a corner. I stopped to inquire what was wrong. He said he was an engineering student at some university in England and that he was cut off from his family in Gaza, which had been overrun by the Israelis. He had come to ask for help at the embassy but was told they could do nothing for him. Penniless, he did not know where to turn. I took his name and telephone number more in a gesture of solidarity than with any clear purpose in mind. Halfway through the dinner with Emile, I remembered the young man and told Emile about him. Without a moment's hesitation, Emile said, "Ring up the boy and tell him I will pay all his expenses until graduation. Tell him also that upon graduation he has an assured job in my company." And so it was. This is a vintage, nearly daily Hasib gesture.

APD was only the first of the nonprofit public benefit corporations of which Hasib became the hub. I was involved, directly or indirectly, with several of those that followed. During 1970–71, the inhabitants of the Gaza Strip had to endure the brutalities of Israeli general Ariel Sharon. Their plight evoked great sympathy in the Arab countries, but little practical help except for the individual efforts of the two Alami brothers, Sami the banker and Samih the doctor, themselves from Gaza. A volunteer group of women was organized by my wife Rasha, Leila Baroudi, and Hala Salaam. They set up office in the basement of our house and sent delegations to the Arab Gulf countries to collect contributions. With these they established the Gaza Students Fund, which offered some thirty scholarships for high school students from Gaza, whom they selected with the help of the Red Crescent. They rented and furnished a hostel to receive them and arranged for their transportation to Beirut. They supplemented this effort with an information campaign that included the observation of a Gaza Solidarity Day among sympathetic, mostly student organizations in fifty cities inside and outside the Middle East.

The concept of a scholarship fund caught on and was expanded to include deserving Palestinian students in general, but this was beyond the means of the Gaza Fund or the Alami brothers. Enter Hasib with his usual largesse. The Gaza Fund and the Alamis joined forces in what became the Palestine Students Fund, with Hasib as chairman. The new fund, incorporated under Lebanese law in 1973, was the first private venture of its kind in the Arab world. It took the Arab League another ten years to establish its own Fund for Students Affected by Catastrophes or War. Contributions were solicited from individuals and governments throughout the Arab world. The Palestine Students Fund is still in operation and has dispensed scholarships to thousands of Palestinian students. Some two decades after its establishment, it inspired the Lebanese multimillionaire (and present prime minister) Rafiq Hariri to establish his own fund for Lebanese students.

Hasib was joined on the board of trustees of the Palestine Students Fund by two "heavyweight" Palestinian philanthropists, Abdul Majid

Shoman, president of the prestigious Arab Bank, and Abdul Muhsin Qattan, the entrepreneur and former speaker of the Palestine National Council. The three were a formidable combination and have been *the* core group for most large-scale Palestinian private philanthropic ventures.

In 1979 Hasib suffered the grievous loss of his wife Diana (née Tamari), to whom he was deeply devoted. He immediately set up a munificent multimillion dollar endowment in her name, the Diana Tamari Sabbagh Foundation, which has since acquired international fame. The objectives of the foundation were to advance medical and educational research; give assistance to hospitals, clinics, universities, and schools; and to alleviate poverty by providing support to needy families. Hasib formed a board of trustees that, apart from himself, included his two sons, his Harvard-trained daughter Sana, the late Khalil Abu Hamad, formerly foreign minister of Lebanon, Drs. Adel Afifi and Samih Alami of the American University Hospital, Abdul Majid Shoman, who became chairman, and myself. The first grants disbursed by the foundation included $5 million to the American University of Beirut—which in gratitude renamed its Basic Sciences Building the Diana Tamari Sabbagh Building—and some $3 million to the universities of the West Bank. Like the APD and the Palestine Students Fund, the Diana Tamari Sabbagh Foundation was a first in the Arab world. Later it would inspire Shoman and Qattan each to establish his own foundation along similar lines in Amman and London, respectively. A cultural subcommittee of the Diana Tamari Sabbagh Foundation under Afifi's competent chairmanship and composed of Dr. Joseph Tamari, Alami, and myself has sponsored almost one hundred individual research projects in the sciences and humanities in the Arab countries, Europe, and the United States.

The establishment of the Diana Tamari Sabbagh Foundation brought us all into close contact with the superbly qualified Palestinian members of the medical staff of the American University Hospital. Drs. Afifi, Alami, and Tamari—as well as Suhail Boulos, Farid Fuleihan, and Samir Azzam—constituted our core medical advisory group. Conclave followed conclave at Hasib's residence in Beirut, interspersed with his contacts with Shoman and Qattan. Gradually, an idea began to crystallize to establish a model hospital in the West Bank. The hospital would have six hundred beds and would become the nucleus of a future national Palestinian university. While the doctors labored over the technical details of the hospital's organization, and we laymen pondered tactics and strategy, Hasib, with the help of Shoman, Qattan, and others bought a plot of land—250,000 square meters—for the site of the future hospital in the village of Sarda, near Ramallah, in the heart of the West Bank.

Israel's invasion of Lebanon in 1982, its pitiless siege of Beirut (a precursor of the Serbian siege of Sarajevo), and the devastation of south Lebanon and the Palestinian refugee camps (some 18,000 civilians, mostly Palestinians, killed, and hundreds of thousands of Palestinians and Lebanese rendered homeless) posed a compelling challenge to the sense of human dignity and worth of Palestinians everywhere.

The scene of our activity now shifted to Hasib's residence in London, where I would visit from the United States, and where we were joined by Basel Aql, who himself had moved to London from Lebanon. Basel, a Palestinian diplomat, had served with the Kuwaiti foreign office and the Arab League Secretariat and had been a PLO volunteer ambassador to the United Nations. He was also a cousin and a former student of mine who, since the mid 1970s, had been associated in Beirut with the political efforts of Hasib and myself (but of this later).

By early July 1982, our ideas began to coalesce around the overriding concept of self-help. The Palestinians in Lebanon needed immediate relief. Their terrible plight should not, however, make us forget our compatriots in the occupied territories or, indeed, in Israel proper. Many Palestinians had done supremely well in helping build up the oil-rich Arab countries. Perhaps a private grant corporation might be set up to enlist their help; only after the corporation was established would we solicit help from the Arab countries themselves.

The corporation, to be set up in Switzerland, would be nonprofit and shun political activity. It would concentrate on economic, social, cultural, and developmental assistance. Donors would comprise three categories: "subscribers," who would contribute an *initial* minimum sum of $100,000; "contributors," who would contribute lesser amounts; and a third category to include selected "intellectuals," who, because of their professional indigence, would be allowed a nominal $500 fee. Only the first and third categories would qualify for membership in the corporation's General Assembly, which would elect its governing board and executive committee.

The rationale behind this seemingly narrow elitist structure was that it would act as an incentive to potential donors while avoiding being perceived as a popular organization in competition with the PLO. The cultural compass of the corporation would include educational and informational activities, particularly in the United States. This last aspect was championed by those of us who resided in the United States—Hisham Sharabi, Edward Said, and myself—who had been appalled by the indifference of the U.S. administration while Beirut burned, particularly during the tenure of Alexander Haig as secretary of state.

These principles were endorsed at two meetings held in London on 9 and 10 July 1982 and attended by a small group that included Sabbagh, Shoman, and Qattan, as well as Aql, businessman Munib Masri, Dalloul, Sharabi, and myself. Sabbagh, Shoman, and Qattan then proceeded to Amman, where the task of rallying subscribers and contributors fell upon Shoman. As chairman of the Arab Bank—the first great successful Palestinian private venture established in the early 1930s by Abdul Majid's legendary father, Abdul Hamid Shoman—he drew upon his immense prestige and credibility in the Palestinian business world. A series of meetings chaired by Shoman in Amman over the next few months was attended by successive groups of donors. In September, the massacres at the Sabra and Shatila refugee camps in Beirut acted as a mighty spur to these efforts. In one meeting, twelve $100,000 subscribers increased their subscriptions to a million dollars each. A whirlwind tour by Sabbagh, Shoman, and Qattan of the Palestinian communities in the Gulf countries followed. By early October, $24 million had been raised. This was deemed sufficient to start operations, and thus the Welfare Association was established in Geneva on 5 October 1982.

Until recently, the Welfare Association was under the capable and dynamic management of George Abed, a senior International Monetary Fund official on loan from his organization, and in whose recruitment I had played a part. The first Arab organization of its kind, in the period 1983 to 1993 the Welfare Association expended some $38 million in grants in Lebanon, the West Bank (including East Jerusalem), the Gaza Strip, and to Palestinians in Israel proper. In addition to emergency relief, these funds were spent on education, economic assistance, and institutional development, in that order.

Welfare itself could not be involved in the educational and informational work in the United States that some of us had urged, but Sabbagh, Shoman, and Qattan were all enthusiastically supportive. Thus the American Middle East Peace Research Institute (AMEPRI) was incorporated in the United States in 1982, with Edward Said, Hisham Sharabi, and Jacob Saliba, an Arab–American businessman, as board members, and myself as advisor. AMEPRI functioned from 1982 until 1986, during which period it supported hundreds of research grants, publications, seminars, and lectures aimed at improving the American public's awareness of the complexities of the Palestine problem and the Arab–Israeli conflict, and the requirements for their peaceful resolution.

The latest public service body with which Hasib and I have been involved is the Center for Muslim–Christian Understanding at Georgetown University in Washington, D.C. The Cold War had ended, and with the disintegration of the Soviet Union, the American dread of communism had abated. But in U.S. quarters grown addicted to having an enemy to fight, withdrawal symptoms set in. In the wake of the Khomeini revolution in Iran and the general resurgence of Islam in the Arab world—itself partly a function of the corruption and ineptitude of the Arab regimes and Arab alienation as a result of Western policies—it was all too easy to pounce on Islam as the new universal threat to Western civilization. This tendency thrived on the virtually total ignorance of the American public about Islam, as well as on the activities in the United States of a few militant extremists who were Muslims.

It is against this background that Hasib and Basel Aql on the one hand and I on the other began thinking about how to address this issue. Concurrently, Georgetown University was interested, as a Catholic institution, in expanding its circle of interreligious ecumenical dialogue. Thus a preliminary meeting was held at Hasib's residence in Washington in 1992, attended by the three of us in addition to Dean Peter Krogh and Professors Ibrahim Ibrahim and Michael Hudson of Georgetown University. Eventually, Hasib conceived of a foundation, incorporated in Switzerland, whose board would include, in addition to himself, Rafiq Hariri, Saudi businessman Sheikh Suleiman Olayan, and others. The foundation would advance the grants that would ensure the launching of the center, whose staff would be comprised of a director and four permanent, term, and visiting professors. All of these would be chosen for their special expertise in Christian–Muslim relations, past and present. The center would offer courses in these fields, which would be integrated into the university's curricula and its School of Foreign Service. The center's program would be guided by an advisory steering committee drawn from the center's faculty, and the department chairs of theology, Arabic, and history. An academic council with Father Bryan Hehir as chair and myself as vice-chair would act as a general advisory body. The university was fortunate in recruiting Professor John Esposito as the director of the center, which has been operating under his dedicated leadership since late 1993.

Yet all these various joint ventures constituted only one part of the "partnership" between Hasib and myself. Another portion involved efforts at political mediation and conciliation. These, too, were self-assumed. Much of their thrust concerned the relations of the PLO with Arab—Lebanese, Syrian, Jordanian, Saudi Arabian—and non-Arab—principally the U.S.—governments. But many of our efforts concerned the major figures within the Lebanese polity itself in the mid-1970s, as well as bilateral relations between some Arab governments—Syrian, Saudi Arabian—and, principally, the United States.

Depending on the nature of the undertaking, our duet sometimes became a trio or a quartet with the addition of either or both Hany Salaam or Basel Aql, the former particularly in the intra-Lebanese field. We operated as a team, complementing one another, pooling our assets, each drawing upon his own network of friends and contacts. Our meetings were held at Hasib's or my house in Beirut and, during the summer, at my house in the mountains in Shemlan. The latter lay on the route between Beirut and Damascus that was taken by the PLO leadership. Chairman Yasir Arafat, who constantly commuted between the two cities and who traveled and worked nocturnally, would not infrequently turn up at Shemlan at two or three o'clock in the morning accompanied by a bodyguard of ten or fifteen tired and hungry fighters expecting to be given dinner or an early breakfast.

Our role was a multiple one, varying in accordance with the protagonist in question, the issue, the personal relationships, the time, and the circumstances. It ranged from mere messenger to representative and advisor and (in the inter-Arab interventions) to confidant and sometimes virtual arbitrator. The number of hours we put into our various mediatory efforts over the course of twenty years was enormous, certainly in the several thousands. I am confident that we did some good and, in certain instances, quite a lot of good, but it would be silly to claim that we had much of an impact on the actual course of events.

In our dealings with the PLO leadership, the person with whom we had the greatest rapport was the late Salah Khalaf (Abu Iyad), second in command of Fatah. Khalaf was originally from Jaffa. He was of a lower-middle-class background and, before becoming a founding member of Fatah in the early 1950s, had earned his living as an Arabic grammar teacher in a secondary school in Kuwait. Khalaf's own formal education was limited, with no university degree or foreign languages, but he had an extraordinarily sharp and well-ordered mind and was richly endowed with common sense. Unlike most politicians, he was a good listener, low-key, soft-spoken, and totally devoid of rhetoric or theatrics. He exuded quiet self-confidence without taking himself too seriously, and had a keen, often self-deprecating sense of humor. Physically, his was an impressive presence; he was of medium height, rather heavily built and with large, sad eyes and bushy eyebrows. For two decades he was our "ally" within the PLO leadership, and, contrary to the hawkish image he projected or the hardline stance attributed to him, his was a major voice in favor of pragmatism, compromise, and moderation in all our efforts with Arafat himself or between Arafat and others, Arab and non-Arab. From the early 1970s onward, he worked behind the scenes in countering Palestinian ideological maximalism and in favor of a resolution of the Palestine problem along the lines eventually endorsed with his public support at the nineteenth Palestine National Council in 1988 in Algiers.

In the early months of the Lebanese civil war, our joint efforts involved mediation between Lebanese leaders. This might, on first glance, seem somewhat odd since neither Hasib nor I was Lebanese by birth. The fact that we were accepted by the leaders concerned was partly due to our status as outsiders, our patent love of Lebanon, and our personal friendships with most of them. Yet it was also due to the conditions prevailing among the Lebanese leaders themselves. Lebanon until the early 1970s was basically a democratic oligarchy presided over by eight or nine major oligarchs who since the 1943 National Covenant had, either themselves or in their earlier incarnations, agreed—however grudgingly and tacitly—to a set pecking order and to the size of each one's (and each one's sect's) portion of the cake. Under the cumulative pressure of domestic, regional, and international developments, and the interaction of these on Lebanese soil, the burden placed upon this system became increasingly unbearable. By the early 1970s, the oligarchy was not only losing grip, but was in rapid decline. One harbinger of the system's collapse was the fact that, as we embarked upon our "shuttle diplomacy" in the spring of 1975, not one of the eight or nine oligarchs was on speaking terms (in the literal sense) with more than one or, at most, two of the others. What we achieved in these conditions was necessarily modest, but we persevered in the conviction that what we were attempting was worth the effort. Nor is it too fanciful to believe that such encouragement as we got from the oligarchs themselves perhaps reflected the secret or unconscious desire of at least some of them for vicarious forthcomingness, where pride and brittle egos prevented their direct cooperation, even in the face of the advancing storm.

One of the roughest days Hasib and I lived through during the Lebanese civil war was 9 December 1975. The previous week had seen a very ugly spiraling of intersectarian incidents. On 1 December, Muslim Kurds had kidnapped twenty Christians in Beirut. On 3 December, Maronite militiamen had seized and burned a truckload of copies of the Quran passing through their neighborhood. Although President Suleiman Frangieh condemned the action, and the mufti of Lebanon urged Muslims not to be provoked, the bodies of five Maronite militiamen were found in Beirut on 6 December. That same day, a Saturday, Maronite militias kidnapped and killed some two hundred Muslims—hence its designation as "Black Saturday." On 8 December, militias of the mostly Muslim opposition launched a large-scale offensive to dislodge Maronite militiamen from their positions in the Beirut hotel district. Following is the entry in my diary from the next day:

9 December 1975: Confusion, and armed men everywhere. About noontime, I am driving my car towards my house. Hasib is next to me. As we pass the former residence of the Egyptian ambassador in the Sana'i quarter, out of nowhere we are surrounded by Lebanese militiamen. They are in a state of great agitation, fingers on the triggers of their Kalishnikovs, thrusting their rifles through the open windows of the car, demanding our

identity cards. One of them, obviously referring to the Maronite militias, is screaming: "They killed my brother, they killed my brother!" Their faces are glistening with perspiration. Meanwhile, Hasib has murmured that he cannot show his identity card because his middle name is patently Christian. I try to address the gunmen in a cool tone: "I am so-and-so. This brother is my friend and guest, and here is my identity card." They grab it, inspect it, and say "Fine. Now let's have the other guy's I.D." I say, "I told you that this brother is my friend and guest. He left his I.D. at home." By this time, the gunmen had begun crowding around Hasib's door, ordering him in loud unison to get out of the car. I say, "You can't do this! And where he goes, I go."

"You keep out of this!" they shout back, and begin trying to force Hasib's door.

Several hands are by now thrust inside the car, wildly clutching at Hasib. Hasib, no lightweight himself, is fending them off while trying to keep the car door shut. I jump out of the car and approach one of the gunmen whose face seemed vaguely familiar, and shout: "Who's your leader? I must talk to the person in charge! This brother and I are advisors to Arafat." Amid the shouting, tugging, and pushing, he motions with his head to a man in middle age about 20 yards away. He is strongly built, quite dark in countenance, almost black. He is ramrod straight, in civilian dress, carrying a Kalishnikov and walking towards us, slowly with *gravitas*. I rush up to him, greet him, and introduce myself and Hasib; the gunmen are now holding back, watching. I say we are advisors to Arafat. He studies my face intently, thinks for a while, and then very quietly, in a Palestinian accent, orders his men to let us go. He chides us, gently, because Hasib is not carrying an I.D., and offers what could be considered one-quarter of an apology. But he releases us, amidst the loud protestations of his gunmen.

Another diary entry, for 14 November 1975, captures a lighter side of our negotiating efforts, albeit against a somber background. At that time, relations between the Sunni prime minister, the late Rashid Karami, and the Maronite president, the late Suleiman Frangieh, had reached a new level of tension. Neither was really seeking a showdown, but each was under mounting pressures from his own constituency and the uncontrollable course of events. The most recent cease-fire, like its numerous predecessors, had broken down. One week earlier there had been two hundred kidnappings by both sides. The opposition—a coalition of leftist and radical groups and militias under the overall leadership of the late Kamal Jumblat—was calling for sweeping reform (including the secularization of the Lebanese system of government) and the resignation of the president. The PLO, though not endorsing the opposition's demands, was nevertheless its de facto ally. On the other side were arrayed the various Maronite groups and militias under the leadership of the late Pierre Gemayel and Camille Chamoun. They were fundamentally in favor of the status quo and advocated strong action by the Maronite-led Lebanese army against both the opposition and, if necessary, the PLO.

Although himself a centrist and a moderate, Karami was nevertheless a hostage of the opposition. He strove for a compromise political solution and was opposed to the use of the army in a repressive role. His position vis-à-vis Frangieh had, however, hardened during the previous few days because of an incident in which a shipload of arms had been delivered to the Maronite militias. Karami had given orders to the army to intercept the ship, but he believed that the army, with the connivance of Frangieh, had allowed it to make its delivery. For several weeks Hasib and I, with the help of Abu Iyad and sometimes Hany Salaam (Basel Aql was away at the United Nations), had been shuttling between Karami and Frangieh to arrange for a *tête-à-tête* between them that might lead to a bilateral understanding on the needed reforms, which they could then jointly endeavor to implement. The ship incident now threatened to destroy all this because, in their mutual exasperation, Karami and Frangieh had decided to take on one another publicly at the ministerial council meeting scheduled for the following day, 15 November. Frangieh was saying he would challenge Karami at the council to present the grievances of the opposition, and Karami was accusing Frangieh of allowing the arms shipment to be delivered to the Maronite militia.

Our group had been greatly perturbed by this turn of events and, with the agreement of Abu Iyad, had decided to try to defuse the looming crisis by persuading Karami and Frangieh to meet with one another to resolve their differences *before* the meeting of the ministerial council the following day. To that end, Salaam had arranged for us—Hasib, himself, and

myself—to meet with Karami at his office at the Ottoman Grand Serai at
10 A.M. My diary for 14 November 1975 reads as follows:

Hasib, Hany, and I enter Karami's office to the sound of heavy firing
outside. . . . I begin a little speech to Karami along the lines we had agreed
upon, entering directly into the substance of the matter: "If major consti-
tutional issues are discussed at tomorrow's ministerial council in this highly
charged confessional atmosphere and with such animus between you and
Frangieh, there will inevitably be an open-ended escalation on both the
political and the security fronts. . . ."

Karami was taking all this in. As is usual when he listens to something carefully, he remains very still, never looking at you directly but
rolling his eyes from side to side, stealing sidelong glances to the distant
corners of the room and, in this case, the high ceilings of the cavernous
Ottoman chamber. At this point Abdallah Yafi [a former prime minister]
is ushered in, red-faced, and in a fluster as usual. We sit out his visit in
silence, myself with mounting impatience, as he drones on in hand-wring-
ing generalities at the sorry state of affairs. Eventually—it is now past
noon and time is running out if a summit between Karami and Frangieh is
to be arranged before the ministerial council tomorrow morning—Yafi
rises to leave. Karami has just returned to his seat after seeing Yafi to the
door. But we had hardly resumed our discussion, when the patriarch of an
Eastern Christian church, wielding his sceptre and accompanied by a whole
covey of priests and deacons in all their ecclesiastical finery, is ushered in.

At this point I give up and say to Hasib: "I am leaving." But he will
not hear of it and, seizing the opportunity of the extended mutual greetings—which remained the gist of the entire ensuing conversation—between
our host and his new guests, he almost physically seizes Hany and me and
leads us to a far corner of the vast room where he insists we should camp
until the departure of the new visitors. The patriarch, in fact, is an old
friend of his and, from our new base, Hasib begins shooting stern and
angry glances in his direction. These having no effect, he presently re-
sorts to a new tactic: at more or less regular intervals, he stands up and in
a perfectly audible voice, addressing as it were no one in particular, de-
claims: "Why don't you just leave and let us finish our discussions with
His Excellency? Nothing that your Holiness can say to His Excellency

could be more important than what we came here to say!" By dint of repetition, this exercise in psychological warfare finally begins to unsettle the prelate who begins to shift uneasily in his chair. Presently, he stands up and with commendable ecclesiastical dignity leads his entourage out of Karami's office and out of earshot.

That day, we prevailed. Karami and Frangieh did meet before the ministerial council session, and the collision toward which they were heading was averted. Alas, this was only a drop of palliative in the swirling tide of doom.

Commenting on the rarity of friends, the philosopher Ralph Waldo Emerson once likened them to a masterpiece of nature. These words have often crossed my mind when thinking of my friendship with Hasib over the years.

There Are Tears in Things

Edward W. Said

I first met Hasib Sabbagh in London during the summer of 1982. He was one of a group of about forty Palestinians who felt impelled to do something serious and concrete to alleviate Palestinian suffering during the ongoing Israeli invasion of Lebanon. Beginning in July of that year, we held a series of group meetings that were to result in the setting up of the Welfare Association, whose offices were later installed in Geneva, where it was officially registered as a Swiss charity. I flew over from the United States for those initial sessions, simultaneously depressed at the horrors taking place three thousand miles away, and impressed at the dispatch and commitment of the business executives and intellectuals who were dedicated to doing their best—without ulterior purpose or hope of reward—for their countrymen and women.

To the best of my knowledge, it was the first time in the modern history of the Arab world that individuals, many of whom had never actually met each other before, came together on their own and on such a scale expressly to contribute money, time, and intellectual effort to what in effect was a moral (albeit at the time a losing) cause. That this purpose involved neither the taking of power nor the expectation of any victory, as that word is normally understood, added to the remarkable quality of the occasion. All of us knew that there was no real way of stopping Israeli

Edward W. Said is University Professor at Columbia University in New York. He teaches English and comparative literature and is the author of "Orientalism," "Culture and Imperialism," "The Politics of Dispossession," and "Representations of the Intellectual."

tanks and planes as they poured their rockets and bombs on an essentially undefended small country that contained a large Palestinian refugee population driven from their land by Zionist forces in 1948. We knew that not as an abstraction, but as part of our own life history—each of us with a family uprooted, years of travail, decades of frustrating work behind us— and we also knew that we had to gather together to act in resistance to this devastating fate we all shared.

Perhaps a dozen of the people in London gradually fell away over time, but a small core group persisted, and Welfare has been the flagship Palestinian organization, with a long record of projects initiated and supported in Lebanon, the West Bank and Gaza, and inside Israel. Hasib has been the heart of the core group, always ready to give money, ready to cajole the reluctant or laggardly, ready to undertake yet one more round of exhausting fundraising. At first, I saw him only at Welfare meetings, but over time we developed a friendship sustained by our common bond in the struggle for Palestine and Palestinian self-determination. Oddly enough, it was only after I had known him for a couple of years that my late mother made me aware that her family, the Bishoutys, who were originally from Safad but had moved to Nazareth in the early part of this century, were actually related to the Sabbaghs, also of Safad. Yet neither she nor Hasib ever elucidated the precise relationship, however, leaving it to Hasib occasionally to say to me with his characteristic humor, "We're related after all!"

Despite the enormous differences between our worlds—Hasib's that of the transnational business tycoon, the realm of politics and influence, of power, and getting things done; mine that of ideas, the university, scholarship, and relative powerlessness—we have communicated through the drive for Palestinian self-determination, as yet unfulfilled and, in my opinion at least, at a tragic impasse. What has amazed me is his unflagging energy, always on the go, never turning down an opportunity to try to better his people's lot no matter how improbable or how great the cost. Once I asked him about his schedule: "London, Athens, the Gulf, Washington, Paris, Geneva, Tunis, Amman, Athens," he answered, all in a matter of days, as if these were places on the board of a parlor game.

Unfailingly, he stays in touch with his friends and acquaintances, more faithful than most to the births, graduations, marriages, illnesses, deaths,

Hasib Sabbagh's house in Beirut during the Israeli invasion of 1982

and successes (or failures) of the friends he telephones, invites out, and is always concerned about. My impression is that his major consideration, more even than his immensely successful business empire, is Palestine, and like a good officer he urges, impels, harangues, and persuades others to go to the front line to do what he has already done. I've never felt that he has expected others to do for Palestine what he has not already been willing to do himself—difficult, draining, and unrewarding though it may be.

Some years ago he told me about the two injunctions given him by his mother. He has tried always to follow these: One is never to turn down someone in need, and the second is never to be disrespectful to an older person. Indeed the range of his support for people and projects is staggering—more impressive than usual because he comes from a tradition where such practices are neither institutionalized nor rewarded—hospitals, libraries, schools, universities, plus ordinary homes and families. All these have benefited from his munificence, which has been offered directly and modestly, without fanfare or pomposity. I think he followed the precept about respect for elders even more assiduously by extending it to respect for people in general. Not given to formality, Hasib, in my view, is one of the most egalitarian of men. He hobnobs with captains of industry or with his friends and family with equal modesty and ease. He never holds a grudge and forgives injuries against him with grace. This in turn obligates people to him, not because of his unending kindness and respect alone, but also because they feel that he is part of their lives, unassuming and unaffected.

For me, the depth of the corresponding sense of obligation he creates in others was inadvertently illustrated when, in the summer of 1992, my family and I traveled to Palestine/Israel. My wife and children had not been there before; I was returning to the places of my birth and early life for the first time in forty-five years. One day, we were in the north, exhausted and hot after several hours of driving through the transformed country. We were expected for lunch in Nazareth and already an hour late when we passed a sign for Safad, some distance off our course. The town had meant something to me as a child, but it was out of our way and the hour was late. Without premeditation, both my wife Mariam and I said to each other, "Let's go there. After all, we couldn't come all this way and not visit Safad. For Hasib's sake!" We did visit after all, although ironically I remembered that I hadn't earlier gotten a description of the family house from Hasib.

My strongest impression about Hasib, however, is based on what I have interpreted as an abidingly sad expression on his face. He can be silent in company, of course, but generally he is affable and engaging. He never speaks of his tremendous achievements, nor does he remind people of how he has helped or contributed so generously. Yet something about his look of composed reflectiveness reveals a kind of sorrow, not at the specific suffering he has so stoically endured along with his people, but a more general kind, rather like Virgil's *sunt lacrimae rerum*—"there are tears in things." Always the doer and the activist, Hasib is more impressive to me because of his perception of the inescapable tragedy of human life. That he has struggled heroically and given to good causes on a grand scale has not diminished what appears to me as his understanding of how rare are the moments of relief, the bright spots in an otherwise dark landscape. His grasp of this is, I think, Hasib's fundamental heroism.

Adversity Can Be Removed

Clovis Maksoud

Although he can be accurately described as an elder statesman on the Arab political scene, Hasib Sabbagh can also be portrayed as a trusting and honest politician. In a paradoxical twist, one can attribute his stature as a statesman to the transparency of his youthful innocence.

As a statesman, Hasib has pursued the role of mediator among contending parties. During the period of his active involvement in the quest for a free Palestinian patrimony, he was, and still continues to be, a conciliator among the Palestinians themselves and between Palestinians and the rest of the Arab nation. Many who mistook his propensity to reconcile for a willingness to compromise eventually realized that their assessment needed urgent revision in light of the developments of 1993 and 1994. While he persists in calling upon his constituency to admit hard and unpleasant facts, he is deferential to and supportive of those who refrain from submission to these realities.

Hasib is among the few of his generation who responds to his first name alone when it is pronounced by his friends, who do so easily but with immense reverence. Another such person is Constantine Zureik, who, at eighty-five years of age, is still being called "Costy" by his students and friends. My late teacher Albert Hourani was always referred to as "Albert." For such persons, names are pronounced with reverence and an expression of endearment. "Hasib" in current political discourse is recognized as Hasib

Clovis Maksoud is director of the Center for the Global South at the American University in Washington, D.C.

Sabbagh, in much the same manner that "Costy" and "Albert" are identified within their own Arab academic and intellectual circles.

Hasib—the successful entrepreneur, contractor, and engineer—sought to transform his business success into a demonstration of what his people could do if given the chance. Throughout his years in the diaspora, he was an example of what might have been had the untapped potential of the Palestinian people been released. Confidence in his people is reciprocated by the affection that the Palestinian people hold for him. For them, he was always there when needed, helping the leadership when his consensus was required and admonishing when necessary. Fearless, courageous, and dedicated, he was also generous, compassionate to a fault, and decent. I refer to decency—which in the vortex of contemporary Arab politics can be risky—to emphasize that Hasib successfully shattered a widespread impression that decency is synonymous with naïveté. He was thus both an example and a catalyst for motivating many principled individuals to become involved and active in the plight of the Palestinians; he has been instrumental in building some of the most successful Palestinian institutions.

When an economic delegation from the Palestine Liberation Organization (PLO) met in Washington, Hasib, as was his custom, invited them to his home. That night, Hasib was so encouraged by their dedication and knowledge that he prodded them to act in accordance with their ethical standards and commitments, irrespective of the adverse political circumstances of the moment. He announced that *they* were the future. Knowing that I was a critic of the PLO–Israeli agreement, he gazed at me and said, "Look at these builders of our new society and not at those you so criticize." At that, his eyes brightened and his smile gave him radiance. In retrospect I can see that Hasib was surreptitiously seeking a new coalition.

Hasib remains forward looking. One can disagree with him—and how often we did—but it is nearly impossible to oppose him. I believe he prefers argumentation as a means of achieving consensus rather than gaining instant consent without any discussion. It is this attitude of his that renders "opposing" him a draining experience.

Palestine—the memory, the legacy, and the identity—is at the core of Hasib's commitment. He believes that every opportunity should be explored, every record preserved, every viable institution assisted, and every door knocked upon. Prejudice should not deter persuasion; adversity can

Hasib Sabbagh and Lebanese president Elias Hirawi exchange greetings, 1995

be removed; every resource should be tapped. This is his creed. Aware as he is of his people's potential—hence his generous contributions and institutional initiatives—he is equally conscious of his people's vulnerability and that of their cause. Knowledge of both the strength and weakness of the Palestinian condition defines Hasib's principled pragmatism.

My relationship with Hasib Sabbagh is as close and friendly as our association is intermittent. He is appreciative of my commitment to the causes he supports, although he seems to feel that my judgment on certain issues is ill-timed as a consequence of a "rejectionist" streak that I sometimes nurture. This has led him to be skeptical of me but never suspicious. That is why our friendship has grown and remained constant. Politically, there is a healthy tension between us and a personal equation that is both comfortable and built on mutual confidence.

My affinity for him originates from familiarity with his core interests, concerns, and beliefs, which are the products of his rich experience. His formative years were spent in Palestine—while his people were being suppressed and their land confiscated—and, later, in Lebanon, at the American University of Beirut (AUB), where a liberal and democratic culture flourished that enabled Hasib to articulate and promulgate his concerns and beliefs. AUB was, and continues to be, for him, a pivotal experience and platform leading to intricate networking and long-lasting partnerships and affiliations. This illustrates the loyalty that AUB inspires among its alumni and also explains the firm support that it elicits from its benefactor and trustee, Hasib Sabbagh.

When we first met, I found Hasib greatly disturbed about the Lebanese civil strife and deeply hurt by the Palestinian–Lebanese conflict that had arisen. He believed that such struggle was unnecessary and damaging to both peoples with whom he felt a genuine sense of belonging. With a coterie of his colleagues, he shuttled back and forth among the various warring factions, all the while prodding, pleading, and persuading in order to terminate the bloodbath and the recklessness; Hasib also attempted to reconcile with both sides a PLO propensity to interfere and an excessive Lebanese sensitivity toward its own sovereignty. Understanding the Palestinian quest for remaining relevant through armed struggle during the 1970s and the fragility of a Lebanese polity based on a precarious communal balance, Hasib was often able to transmit each party's anxieties and legitimate concerns from one to the other. This was a daunting task, yet he shouldered it willingly because he realized that a Palestinian–Lebanese breach could only increase their joint vulnerability. What might follow (and did follow) was in effect such a fissure, deepened by the Israeli invasion of Lebanon in 1982 and the Palestinian dispersal that ensued.

In the early 1980s I came to know Hasib more closely because of my position as the ambassador of the Arab League to both the United Nations and the United States. At that time, I knew *of* him more than I actually knew him. I recall his philanthropic endeavors, his construction firm, the professionalism of his enterprises, his love for and devotion to his wife, whose untimely death affected him so profoundly, his services to his extended family, his stature among various Arab and international leaders, and the esteem in which he was widely held. These dimensions of the man were common knowledge when I started seeing him more frequently.

He thought I was a bad bridge player; perhaps he had a better impression of me as a political bridge builder. Once, with the late ambassador of Jordan, Mohammed Kamal, I was asked to cut the ribbon at the opening of a branch of the Arab Bank Limited in New York. Hasib was a member of the bank's board of directors and attended the ceremony. He suggested that the Arab League open a bank account; I responded both to him and to the bank's chairman, Abdul Majid Shoman, that if all accounts being solicited were like the Arab League's—given its dire financial straits—there would be no need to cut the ribbon.

Taking this hint, Hasib asked me a few days later how he could assist the myriad Arab–American organizations that were defending Palestinian rights and Arab aspirations in the United States. Hasib was cognizant of the growing importance of the role of the United States in the Middle East, and he was eager in particular for Palestinians to have credible access to U.S. policymakers and decisionmakers. The network of contacts he established was equipped to introduce the question of Palestine to the public at a time when the PLO was shunned and its presence illegal.

Recognizing the unfairness of the PLO's exclusion, Hasib and his political friends persisted in pressing their cause through active intellectual and scholarly avenues. He was instrumental in opening a branch of the Beirut-based Institute of Palestine Studies in the United States, contributing to fellowships at major universities, and promoting cultural events. Official Washington was impressed, although the impact for which Hasib and his friends had hoped would continue to elude them. While Hasib resists the temptations of grandiose theater, such as that which took place on the White House lawn on September 13, 1993, there are other ways in which Hasib has worked for a Palestinian–American rapprochement; he has worked equally hard to sustain Palestinian dignity.

For Hasib, the Oslo agreement represented a new opening, but transparency and political accountability among the Palestinian leadership was the more crucial priority. Even as this volume was being compiled, Hasib was troubled but motivated, anxious yet hopeful, helpful while restrained, and generous although with conditions. He and many of his business associates are keen to invest in their patrimony, both to prove their mettle and rebuild their society in the occupied Palestinian lands. This is being instituted slowly, notwithstanding the fact that lingering skepticism regarding the PLO leadership delays their thrust and a continuing suspicion of Israeli occupation policies persists.

Hasib's experience with the Geneva-based Welfare Association demonstrates his keenness to build and to explore opportunities for both social and business investment. In pursuing his many objectives and in authenticating a credible Palestinian presence, Hasib has worked with the Carter

Center, Harvard University, and, most recently, with Georgetown University, where he founded and funded the Center for Muslim–Christian Understanding. What prompted him in the Georgetown endeavor was a perception that Islam was under attack and that, for some in the United States, Muslim extremism had become synonymous with Islam; the image of Islam was becoming distorted, and many rights of Muslims were being denied. The historic reality of Islam as both a faith and a civilization was unrecognizable in the prevailing discourse. Hasib Sabbagh felt that this development represented an impending threat to Arab–American understanding that, if allowed to continue, would poison the relations of the United States with its own growing Muslim population and the rest of the Muslim world. Rectification was overdue, he felt. One of the best Islamic scholars was entrusted with the new center's direction, John Esposito. I was present at the establishment of the institution, but when Hasib had sought my advice I had expressed reservations because I feared that the very presumption of misunderstanding might worsen the situation. I also believed that when such a presumption exists, one's conviction must be that it is temporary. I realize now that the intensity of what appears in retrospect to have been a campaign against Islam gives credence to Hasib's theory, yet I am still not convinced. While I maintain reservations about presuming that misunderstanding abounds, I support the center's programs for their intrinsic worth, and Yvonne Haddad's association with the institution reinforces my faith in its usefulness.

In Hasib Sabbagh, one discovers characteristics that make us hopeful and optimistic that the Arabs, too, in the words of the American civil rights movement and Martin Luther King, Jr., "shall overcome." The pain that Hasib felt during the 1991 Gulf War and during the latest civil strife in Yemen was both visible and touching. His eagerness and efforts to mobilize people to avoid conflicts, or stop them, have brought me even closer to him. On issues that wound our collective conscience, as on others, Hasib the humanist is at his best. In one sense, his continuous quest for avoidance of conflict, or resolution when they occur, are akin to the very qualities that make Hasib's friend Jimmy Carter a great former president—as the events of 1994 in both North Korea and Haiti have proven him to be.

Although our opinions have differed at times, Hasib's and my purposes and commitments have remained the same throughout our relationship. This mutual trust has sealed our ties and made of them the underpinnings of an ever-growing friendship. Hasib's misgivings with regard to some of my opinions continue to be an incentive for me to sharpen my wits in hopes that someday, twenty-five years from now, he might telephone a ninety-year-old Clovis and say, "You were right."

Basel Aql, Hasib Sabbagh, Pope John Paul II, Leo J. O'Donovan, S.J., and Cardinal Francis Arinze at the Vatican, 1993

One Day of Memory

Leo J. O'Donovan, S.J.

It has been my pleasure to have known Hasib Sabbagh for several years and, so, I am both honored and humbled to be among those who join to honor him in this volume. Hasib and I have talked often at Georgetown University; we have dined together in Washington and Rome, and we have exchanged stories about the cities where we were born and countries we have visited. Yet the focus of our friendship has been the establishment at Georgetown University of the Center for Muslim–Christian Understanding. Hasib conceived of this remarkable endeavor as a crowning achievement of his life.

At the oldest Roman Catholic university in the United States and in our nation's capital, Hasib has seen to the establishment of a hub for the study and teaching of the intricate, multifaceted, and centuries-old interrelationship of the Christian and Islamic worlds. With the participation of close friends, he has committed himself to deeper understanding, religious harmony, and the hope for peace, grounded not merely in the absence of hostility but also in the presence of mutual appreciation and admiration. The project could not have been more timely, nor could Georgetown University have been more pleased about the commitment of Hasib and his friends that the center be forever a place in Washington from which learning serves justice and peace throughout the world.

Hasib and I were both in Washington on September 13, 1993, when the historic Declaration of Principles was signed by representatives of Israel and the Palestine Liberation Organization on the South Lawn of the

---

Leo J. O'Donovan, S.J., is president of Georgetown University in Washington, D.C.

White House. That event gave impetus for our center to include religious dialogue with Judaism. In this, both of us were encouraged by the vigorous agreement of Hasib's generous daughter Sana. Hasib addressed the point directly in his gracious remarks at the reception following the inaugural ceremonies for the opening of the center.

Among my many memories of working with Hasib on this seminal effort, none is more vivid than our private audience with Pope John Paul II. Traveling together to the Vatican on a brilliant spring day in 1993, Hasib and I were received by the pope and enjoyed a lively conversation describing the project for Muslim–Christian understanding at Georgetown. With his well-known concern for strengthening relationships between Christianity and Islam, and his personal dedication to that conversation, the pope expressed vivid interest in our plans and warmly commended them. We were also pleased and grateful to receive at the conclusion of the audience his personal blessing for the center, which took on new gravity and fulfillment at that very moment.

My memory of that May day shines even more than others when I think of the man who is honored in this volume, yet it is also true that one day of memory in a human being possesses vitality for us through its connection with all the other days of our experience. Thus I offer these few words with the heartfelt and fond wishes for a lover of his people, a distinguished citizen of the world community, a benefactor and true friend of Georgetown, and, for me personally, a man whom I greatly admire.

The Impossible Simply Takes A Little Longer

Peter F. Krogh

One goes through life hearing about rare individuals whose capacities and accomplishments are larger than life. They loom behind the scenes initiating grand enterprises and endowing them with a vision and energy that transcends the commonplace. Singlehandedly—through the sheer force of their aspirations—they embolden the field around them and raise everything to a higher standard. Such a man is Hasib Sabbagh.

For years prior to our first meeting, I had felt and been affected by the presence of Hasib Sabbagh in the broad field of international affairs, in which I had worked for one-third of a century. A legend in his own time, redoubtable businessman, intrepid advocate of justice, magnanimous and resourceful philanthropist, he appeared to be a rare specimen of humankind: universally respected and regarded with an admixture of respect and awe. I stood among those who recognized the remarkable quality and extent of his influence but who had not met him. He verged on being a mythical character along Herculean lines, and I wondered when would I meet the man behind the fable?

The occasion to do so presented itself in the form of an initiative that by its very nature and magnitude bespoke the legend. In the autumn of 1992, I was informed through a mutual friend, Basel Aql, that Hasib Sabbagh wished to establish a center for Muslim–Christian understanding at Georgetown University. I was advised that he wanted the project to be

Peter F. Krogh is dean of the Edmund A. Walsh School of Foreign Service at Georgetown University in Washington, D.C.

mounted immediately, and at a level of quality and scope that would establish it almost overnight as the premier center of its kind in the world. Hasib Sabbagh planned to seize the moment of careless and potentially self-fulfilling talk about a clash of civilizations to launch an educational effort that could obviate the contest. I was informed that I should make myself available to dine with Hasib Sabbagh at his Washington residence to discuss the project. I was all too pleased, indeed, eager, to do so.

I arrived at the appointed hour at the Sabbagh home, adjacent to the Austrian ambassadorial residence, and was met at the door by the legend himself. He seemed a gruff man, compacted by a half-century of hard labor in a tough neighborhood, wearing a suit that would have fit him well had he been (as he once was) two inches taller. Silently, he escorted me to a sofa adjacent to his favorite chair and spent what seemed like an eternity working his worry beads, staring me in the eyes, wordlessly taking my measure. Servants relieved the scene with service, and Basel rescued me with friendly chatter. I looked down at my watch believing that fifteen minutes had passed to find that only three minutes had elapsed. Then it happened. He smiled. It was the smile of a shy person, a modest person, a deeply private but caring person. It was a sensitive smile, vulnerable and honest. I raised my gaze from his lips to his eyes and there flashed another beacon—a twinkle in his eyes, a sign of playfulness merged with audacity, a summons to a foray that commingled adventure, significance, and good fun. We started to talk, to share experiences and insights, reciprocally gauging our common interests and the reach of our imaginations. Yet so economical was the conversation, so targeted to bedrock values, that I believe I can say, without exaggeration, that within a real (rather than imagined) fifteen minutes, we became trusted friends.

There followed a conversation more like a negotiation over a period of weeks that produced the foundation for an educational edifice designed to thwart the putative clash of civilizations. Hasib believed that ignorant and self-interested elements in the world could, if left to their own devices, replace the Cold War with the heat of confessional conflict. The casualties would be peace and progress, particularly in the regions cohabited by Christians and Muslims. Hasib felt strongly that persons of peace were duty bound to work *proactively* to reduce the risk of such conflict. He wished to put his money where his mouth was by constructing an educational bulwark against confessional misunderstanding and intolerance. To this end, Hasib, with assistance from like-minded associates, assembled an endowment, created a foundation, and challenged Georgetown University with his unwavering support to make his vision a reality.

As the midwife for this enterprise, I was witness to and partner in an audacious endeavor of breathtaking pace from conception to implementation. Hasib wanted the project launched immediately and at a world-class level. His impatience with academic customs and bureaucracy was equaled by his determination not to be foiled by them and vastly exceeded by his generosity. Within six months from our first meeting, and with indefatigable and resourceful assistance from Basel, a charter for a comprehensive center had been crafted and signed, a prestigious director appointed, and the construction of a physical home for the new entity commissioned and funded. In one quarter of a century of building entrepreneurial institutions in the international field, I had never witnessed, much less been a party to, such a swift and sure act of creativity.

Hasib's enterprise now commands the heights in its field. Its director, John Esposito, is editor-in-chief of the four-volume *Oxford Encyclopedia of the Modern Islamic World*. The appointed faculty that joined Esposito at the Center for Muslim–Christian Understanding are household names in their fields. Overnight, the endeavor has become the venue for informed and highly influential public-affairs discussions of Islamic–Christian relations. An endowed chair of Southeast Asian Islam has been contributed by Malaysian backers and a chair of South Asian Islam waits immediately in the wings. A suite of offices houses the center in an addition to the university's Intercultural Center. The reality of the new venture is moving straight ahead in the direction of Hasib's vision, to the great benefit of humankind.

Hasib Sabbagh has made his fortune primarily in construction in the Middle East, yet he has assured his place in history by being a builder on a grand scale in the world at large. Professionally, he commands a vast construction empire grounded in bricks and mortar and conducted on the premise that the impossible simply takes a little longer. Personally, he commands a vision of humanity rooted in a commitment to justice and pursued on the premise that with equity comes hope. Ultimately, therefore, Hasib Sabbagh is a creator and constructor of hope. A man of deep faith, he is an exemplar of that touchstone of civilizational progress.

At the Vatican, Hasib Sabbagh meets Pope John Paul II, while accompanied by Michel Sabbah (center), the current Latin patriarch of Jerusalem, and Patriarch Maximos Hakim (far right), 1981

A Man and His Vision

John L. Esposito

Who is Hasib Sabbagh? This was my response when I first heard the name. I was soon to learn about Hasib's many friends in the Middle East and the West and about his international impact. My connection with the businessman and philanthropist, therefore, is relatively recent, the result of a shared concern and mission.

During the summer of 1993, Father J. Bryan Hehir, then vice president of Georgetown University, asked me to meet him for lunch near my home in Wayland, Massachusetts. During our meal, he indicated that Georgetown had been approached about establishing a center for Muslim–Christian understanding. We spent the better part of lunch in a wide-ranging discussion about the needs and benefits of such a center, its potential competitors, and the scope of its work. After Bryan left, I moved on with my work and proceeded to forget about our discussion. The idea resurfaced and became more of a reality in October of that same year, in Washington, when I was attending a meeting of the National Conference of Catholic Bishops' Consultation on Catholic–Muslim Relations and conducting radio interviews to promote my book, *The Islamic Threat: Myth or Reality?* While there, a telephone message was left at my Massachusetts home from Father Patrick Heelan, the executive vice president of Georgetown University. When I called his office, indicating that I was in Washington, he hastily invited me to meet that afternoon with him and Peter F. Krogh, the dean of the School of Foreign Service.

John L. Esposito is director of the Center for Muslim–Christian Understanding at Georgetown University in Washington, D.C.

Following up on my talk with Bryan Hehir, Father Heelan and Dean Krogh again wanted to discuss a proposal that I now learned had come from the Foundation for Christian–Muslim Understanding in Geneva. The center the foundation wanted to create would focus on Muslim–Christian relations in international affairs. My initial reaction to the idea was positive, but qualified. While such a center could fill an important need, there already were several well-known centers—the MacDonald Center at Hartford Seminary and that at Selly Oaks College in England. It was important that we not simply duplicate or compete with established programs. I had been in academia too long not to be wary of the tendency of some schools to develop programs that either mirrored already existing resources or lacked a sufficiently distinctive vision and mission to make them worthwhile. When I heard about the potential donors and their proposed vision for the center, however, I could not believe it. It was as if they had identified the core issues of my own work and all of my current concerns. We seemed to share a strong conviction about the troubling relationship between the Muslim world and the West. In particular, we agreed that with the demise of the Soviet Union, Islam should not be regarded as the new threat. To address this issue, we discussed a center whose research and teaching—and especially public-affairs programs and activities—would address the historic relationship of Islam and Christianity as well as that of the Muslim world and the West. As we talked, it became clear that the evolving focus of such a center complemented that of the university, as the president, executive vice president, and dean of the School of Foreign Service were aware of the role of religion in international affairs in general and concerned about the implications of mutual understanding between Muslims and Christians in particular.

During this first meeting, I functioned primarily as a consultant, responding to a variety of queries: Where are the major existing centers? Is there a need for a new center? What should such a center look like? What should be the role of center faculty? As I reflect on the meeting, I remember my growing excitement. As we continued, it became difficult to contain my enthusiasm concerning the significance and timeliness of such a center's mission. Hasib Sabbagh—at that time I still had little idea of the man and the foundation he represented—and the university were proposing not simply one more center, but an "idea whose time has come." As we were to say many times later, the center embodied "the right idea, in the right place, at the right time." I had been told that we only had one hour for our meeting, due to Father Heelan's schedule. Yet, in his enthusiasm, he continued to extend our meeting, several times asking "one last question." Finally, just as it seemed that the conversation was over, Father Heelan and Dean Krogh asked if my wife and I could move to Washington. The question caught me completely off guard, but my spontaneous response was, "We very well might be moveable!"

I was later pleased to learn that at an early stage in their conversations about the creation of a center, when the university's representatives—Father Heelan and Dean Krogh—had discussed the nature of the director's position with Hasib, both had identified me as their candidate. As the perhaps apocryphal story goes, Hasib produced copies of my books—*Islam: The Straight Path* and *The Islamic Threat: Myth or Reality?*—and declared, "This is the person we need." After our first personal encounter, which followed shortly after this meeting, I realized that Hasib was in agreement with much of what I had written.

My first private session with Hasib took place in London; I was on a business trip and took the opportunity to meet him for dinner. We dined that evening at the home of Basel Aql, his associate, good friend, and business associate. The evening was memorable for it revealed some of the many facets of our host: the spectacular view of the park where he and Hasib often enjoyed an hour's walk together, portraits of Palestine that reflect his innermost identity, and an impressive personal library that would be the envy of any academic. I was at this point very interested in getting a better idea of Hasib as a man, as well as the purpose and goals of his foundation. I also wanted to give both of us a chance to see if we really had a meeting of the minds and whether we could work effectively together. Although I knew that the center would be independent, I believed that the foundation, as well as the university, should have confidence in the founding director. To be honest, I had previously decided that I'd had my fill of administration. It didn't make sense to move on to become director of this center unless such an assignment represented the opportunity to be part of something fresh and worthwhile that could make a significant contribution.

I had been forewarned that Hasib Sabbagh was a person of few words who would often sit and listen, saying little. Basel was frequently known to carry the conversation. To my surprise, however, barely had we sat down and begun our discussion than Basel disappeared. With some apprehension, I looked over at Hasib. I continued the conversation, which centered on my background and training, describing how an Italian Roman Catholic from Brooklyn came to the study of Islam in the late 1960s and early 1970s. We talked about travels in the Muslim world, research interests, and projects. In particular, we spoke of the need to improve the West's understanding of Islam and to address issues that threatened to undermine the relationship of Islam and the West. Emphasis on conflicts and differences, we agreed, should be offset by an awareness and acknowledgment of the common beliefs and values that Christians, Muslims, and Jews share. All are Children of Abraham—"People of the Book"—and all worship the one God, acknowledge God's prophets and revelations, believe in human responsibility and accountability, and in eternal reward and punishment.

We talked about the international dimension and implications of Muslim–Christian relations, as the realities of our globally interdependent world reinforce even more today the need for mutual understanding and recognition of that which unites us rather than divides us. We spoke of how stereotypes of a militant Islam and a Crusader West were being reinforced by the impact of the Iranian Revolution, the holding of American and other hostages in Iran and Lebanon, news media exploitation of terrorist activities, and the tendency during the 1980s to elevate Qadhdhafi's Libya and Khomeini's Iran alongside the Soviet threat. These images, we noted, fostered mistrust and suspicion, resulting in strained relations from the equation of Islam with extremism and terrorism, talk of clashing civilizations, and fears of an impending confrontation between the Muslim world and the West. Such distortions of reality threaten Muslim–Christian and international affairs we noted, and, with the breakup of the Soviet Union, Hasib and I were concerned that the "threat vacuum" not be filled by the projection of an alternative global menace, and that Islam not be unfairly equated with "Islamic fundamentalism," extremism, and terrorism.

Hasib continued to engage me in an animated conversation for sometime, telling me of his dream for the center and how it was to address many of the issues and concerns that we had identified. Though we were individuals with very different backgrounds, we discovered our common commitment to countering dangerous stereotypes and promoting better understanding. Hasib's passion for the subject did not spring from the soul of a romantic idealist, but from the rich experience of a realist who traveled constantly throughout the region and was in regular contact with leaders in the Muslim world and the West. I remember being particularly struck by something he said, and would say again many times afterwards. Hasib talked about his desire to give something back and of his awareness that he had been extremely successful and fortunate in his business life. He, an Arab Christian, had benefited and prospered from his long association and dealings with many Arab Muslim leaders and countries. He now wished to provide something enduring to the Arab world from which he came and in which he had prospered. As he had lived and done business in a world in which Christians and Muslims worked side by side, so, too, he wanted to counter those forces that contributed to undermining that spirit of cooperation and mutuality. He and the other donors to the foundation represented this spirit of mutual understanding—half were Christian and half were Muslim. Hasib saw that isolated events and the actions of individual groups had created a climate of suspicion that threatened Muslim–Christian relations not only regionally, but also globally, having serious political and economic implications. Thus, Hasib commented, the creation of a center would address relations between the Muslim world and the West, both in Washington and internationally, and would be a major legacy to which he would devote his time and energies.

It was at this point in our conversation that I saw another side of Hasib—the decisive, no-nonsense decisionmaker. As we moved to the dining-room table, he turned to me and said, "So, when can you start!" Flabbergasted, I responded that this was just a preliminary conversation designed to enable us to get to know each other and see if we shared a common vision . . . that I really hadn't decided whether I was ready to make the move . . . and, in any case, the university had not made a formal offer. Hasib listened quietly to my explanation, but the look on his face grew more and more incredulous. Given his passion for the creation of the center, it was clear this was not an answer he expected. He was ready to make it happen!

My visit with Hasib revealed two characteristics that would reemerge on many occasions. First, he had a defined vision of the need for and a powerful commitment to Muslim–Christian understanding, and second, like any successful businessman, once he saw his goal, he was confident he could achieve it and expected it to be done "yesterday."

CREATION OF THE CENTER

After my return from London, Hasib and the university moved quickly. A number of names for the center had been suggested. As we moved toward wording such as the "Center for Muslim–Christian Relations," Basel informed us that, whatever we decided, Hasib was adamant that one word be in the title: *understanding.* We finally decided upon a rather cumbersome appellation, but one that reflected both the mission and scope of the institution, the Center for Muslim–Christian Understanding: History and International Affairs (CMCU). The center's two foci were to be the historic relationship of Islam and Christianity and the relationship of the Muslim world and the West. Our mission combined the fields of religion, history, and international affairs.

Before I had even completed my contract with the university, Hasib moved rapidly in the late spring of 1993 formally to complete the signing of the agreement creating the center, and he hosted several luncheons to launch the institution. These meetings took place at his home and, again, revealed much about the donor. Hasib is not only a modern corporate leader, but also a traditional Arab patriarch. His meetings are always conducted over a generous, if not sumptuous, lunch or dinner at his home, over which he *presides.* The seating of each guest and the pace and focus of the conversation to the conclusion of the meal are overseen by Hasib as head of the family. At the end of a luncheon or dinner meeting, it is not uncommon for him to give guests a travel bag embossed with his company's logo, CCC, and filled with wonderful sweets and pistachio clusters from the Middle East and exquisite cigars. Indeed, Hasib introduced us to his cigars by presenting them to Leo J. O'Donovan, S.J., president of Georgetown University, and when he learned that I enjoyed cigars, I was luckily included as a regular recipient of what some would call the "best cigars in the world." Although I had long given up smoking, his cigars proved to be unique, and I found myself planning special walks dedicated to enjoying them.

I had been advised that Hasib had a computer-like mind that stored information, and thus he was able to act with no need for notes or reminders. This, indeed, seems to be the case. It is well illustrated by the manner with which he leads each conversation, moving from one concern or item of business on his mental list to another, remembering the details of decisions made. Hasib's mental powers are complemented by a no-nonsense realism. Around Hasib, small talk is usually replaced by more substantive concerns. Increasingly during our interactions, two themes prevailed, both seeming now to be his major passions: a just peace for Palestine and the launching of the center and its work.

Implementation of a Vision: CMCU

The Center for Muslim–Christian Understanding: History and International Affairs officially opened in September 1993, with a mission to foster the study of Muslim–Christian relations and to promote better understanding and dialogue between the Muslim world and the West. The center combines teaching and research at the undergraduate and graduate levels, with an emphasis on public-affairs activities, both nationally and internationally. Our audience is not only the academic and religious communities, but also the broader community of actors in international affairs, extending from policymakers and government officials to journalists and corporate leaders. Thus, the United States—specifically its capital, Washington, D.C.—and Georgetown University proved to be an ideal location for the work of the center. The political, military, and cultural influence of the United States and the impact of the U.S. media in the Arab and broader Muslim worlds provide Washington an incomparable vantage point.

Georgetown University offers the center its location in a major university with high visibility in the United States and in international affairs. Georgetown, founded in 1789, is the nation's oldest Catholic and Jesuit university. It enrolls 12,084 students from fifty states and 110 foreign countries in its nine schools. Essential dimensions to the life of Georgetown University—its religious heritage and ecumenical character, as well as its engagement in international affairs—provide the foundation upon which CMCU was developed.

Both its Catholic–Jesuit heritage and its location in Washington have shaped Georgetown's abiding interest in the study of international relations. In particular, Georgetown is the home of the Edmund A. Walsh School of Foreign Service, the oldest and largest school of international affairs in the United States. Established in 1919, the school celebrated its seventy-fifth anniversary in 1994–95. It conducts an undergraduate program for 1,300 students and a master's program for 120 students. The Walsh School includes the Center for Contemporary Arab Studies, fast approaching its twenty-fifth anniversary, a major resource for interpreting and understanding the Arab world, and one which enjoys great visibility throughout the Middle East. Georgetown's faculty—scholars and diplomats—have been major interpreters and players in the history and politics of the Muslim world and the West. Graduates have included senior U.S. government officials and diplomats—from President Bill Clinton to assistant secretaries of state—as well as many scholars, diplomats, and corporate leaders of the Muslim world.

At Georgetown, the Catholic tradition has been fostered in an ecumenical and interreligious context. With the creation of CMCU, Georgetown committed itself substantially to expanding the teaching and research of the Islamic tradition that already existed at the university. The Center for Muslim–Christian Understanding benefits from and draws upon the university's existing curricular and human resources. The university has developed academic programs in Christian and Jewish studies, offered particularly in the Department of Theology. A base of course offerings in Islamic studies are to be found within the Center for Contemporary Arab Studies and in the Arabic, theology, and history departments.

The vision of Hasib Sabbagh and of Georgetown University could not have been more timely and relevant. Islam is one of the great spiritual and social forces in the world today; its influence and significance will grow and develop in the twenty-first century. The religious, social, regional, and international significance of Islam—from the Middle East to Central Asia to Africa and South Asia—is a fact of international life. Understanding this truth, relating it to other dimensions of world affairs, and connecting it to the role of Christianity in the world is a central academic theme of CMCU's program. The study of Islam and Muslim–Christian relations at Georgetown encompasses their religious content, cultural significance, and role in international affairs. As an academic inquiry, therefore, the program of CMCU focuses on understanding the intrinsic meaning and significance of Islam, the interaction of Islam with Christianity, and its impact upon Muslim–Christian relations. Both Christianity and Islam take shape in the world as social and institutional forces. The center embodies the need for more extensive research and understanding of how Islam and Christianity relate to each other and their mutual potential to contribute to social justice, peace, and freedom.

The need for CMCU can be seen in the response to its creation. In its first year, more than 1,500 phone calls were received from across the United States and internationally. With a startup staff consisting of the director and an administrative assistant, Patricia Gordon, and with the assistance of Professor Yvonne Y. Haddad from the University of Massachusetts, who was Visiting Research Professor in the spring of 1994, endeavors were undertaken that resulted in an activities report of some twenty pages.

From its inception the center expanded courses for undergraduate and graduate students at the university, developed programs on Islam and the history of Muslim–Christian relations, and organized major international and national conferences and colloquia. New courses in comparative studies have been introduced: "Religion and International Affairs," "Gender, Culture and Islam," "Islam and Politics" "Muslim Communities in the West," and "Islam in Africa." A broad array of public-affairs activities and national and international programs have sought to interpret Islam and the Muslim world to the diverse communities of Washington and abroad. The range of issues is reflected by some of the colloquia topics: "Children of Abraham: Muslim–Christian–Jewish Relations," "Daughters of Sara and Hagar: Religion and Feminism in Judaism, Christianity, and Islam," "Islam, Democracy, and Pluralism," "Muslims on the New Sino–Central Asian Frontier: Ethnic Identities and Religious Nationalisms," "Jerusalem and the Future of Arab Christianity," "The Political Future of Jerusalem," and "Liberation Theology."

The center has co-sponsored major conferences, among them "Political Islam in the Middle East: Its Regional and International Implications," in collaboration with the U.S. Institute of Peace; a series of colloquia on religion and politics with the Carnegie Endowment for Peace; a series of congressional luncheon briefings on "Islam in Africa and U.S. Foreign Policy," in collaboration with the American Muslim Council and Churches for Middle East Peace; and "Religion, Politics and International Relations," co-sponsored with the National Conference of Catholic Bishops. The center has been a major presence at congressional hearings and briefings for senior government officials in the United States, Europe, and the Middle East, the North Atlantic Treaty Organization, multinational corporations, and for religious leaders. Cooperative relationships have been established with universities and centers in Europe, the Middle East, and Asia. The activities of the center and its staff have been covered by the major news media, both nationally and internationally. Press coverage has included the *New York Times, Wall Street Journal, Washington Post, Chicago Tribune, San Francisco Chronicle,* and *Philadelphia Inquirer,* as well as major newspapers in Europe, Japan, the Middle East, and South and Southeast Asia. Since its inception, the center has been joined by visiting professors Nasrin Hakami from the University of Tehran and Fathi Osman, a distinguished Egyptian professor and former editor of *Arabia,* as well as Rashid G. Abdoullaer of Tajikistan.

THE FUTURE

The commitment of Hasib Sabbagh to CMCU is also reflected by his family. Early in the first year of our existence, Hasib's daughter Sana donated $1 million to fund the Hasib Sabbagh Suite, offices that would come to house the center. The new space enabled us to move out of our cramped, temporary space into a new wing of the Intercultural Center, where our neighbors are the Center for Contemporary Arab Studies. The offices provide adequate room for faculty, research associates, and staff. Our move into our new quarters, in December 1994, came at the right time. The vision of Hasib Sabbagh had by the end of our first year not only generated more program opportunities than originally anticipated, but also more faculty. In addition to the director and two permanent faculty positions—for Arab Islam/Muslim–Christian Relations and Arab Christianity/Christian–Muslim Relations, both funded by the foundation—the university in its continued support gave us an additional position in Islamic studies. Our good fortune continued with a totally unexpected capstone event—a chair in Southeast Asian Islam. During the spring of 1995, a group of Malaysian businessmen donated $2 million to create the Malaysia Chair in Southeast Asian Islam. The signing of the final agreement for this additional endowment took place in October 1994—more than an appropriate way to begin our second year! Most importantly, the creation of this chair signified the center's concern with the length and breadth of the Muslim world.

CONCLUSION

Hasib Sabbagh has lived and continues to live a rich and full life. While many lead one-dimensional lives, his is clearly multidimensional. He has not been content simply to enjoy the fruits of success, but has been dedicated to improving the world in which he lives and, more specifically, improving the lives of others. His contributions to the development of the Arab world and to the achievement of an enduring peace in the Middle East are incalculable. He has brought that same level of vision, energy, and commitment to Muslim–Christian relations. A man of two worlds, he has sought to bridge them through the creation of the Foundation for Christian–Muslim Understanding in Geneva and the establishment of the Center for Muslim–Christian Understanding at Georgetown. In the short time I have known him, I have seen Hasib's single-minded dedication to this project. He brings to it an energy and intensity that are formidable, and his tenacity ensures successful results. I was reminded again of all of these qualities recently.

On October 7, 1994, Hasib attended an award ceremony at Georgetown University. President Leo J. O'Donovan presented the President's Medal to Anwar Ibrahim, deputy prime minister of Malaysia. By coincidence, Hasib was in Washington on business and was able to attend. Anwar Ibrahim's acceptance speech was a tour de force. He countered those who warn of an inevitable clash of civilizations and, instead, persuasively and self-critically spoke of the need for civilizational dialogue. As I sat at the front of the room watching the audience react, it was heartening to note Hasib's expression. He was moved and impressed by Anwar Ibrahim. At the end of the speech, Hasib made his way to Anwar to express his agreement. In contrast to those who warmly thanked the deputy prime minister for his comments, Hasib not only praised but also pointedly encouraged Anwar to take, indeed, to *preach,* his message throughout the Muslim world. He then turned to me, noting that Anwar Ibrahim should travel as a roving ambassador and deliver his message, so important to Muslim–Christian understanding. Both in his comments to Anwar Ibrahim and to me, I heard the clear Sabbagh tendency to say "Do it!"

Hasib has spent a lifetime encouraging productive actions in business and politics and has provided a legacy whose impact is incalculable. Knowing the man, there will be more to come as he travels incessantly across the globe and continues to make things happen.

A Professional Man

George P. Shultz

Hasib Sabbagh epitomizes the best of the junction of business success with government policy. On the one hand, I know him as an astute and creative businessman and a fine partner in many joint undertakings. In my role as president of Bechtel, I had the privilege of working with him: he was reliable; he did what he said he would do; you could count on it. The Palestinians that he brought on the job were industrious and excellent workers. That is the image of Palestinians that I have always carried in my mind: constructive, energetic, and intelligent. Hasib Sabbagh has all these same traits.

He also has given his immense energy and intelligence to political issues. He sought to deepen his own understanding of Middle Eastern developments and to help others do so as well. The "others" have included kings, prime ministers, and other political leaders—including at least one U.S. secretary of state. He is a tireless and responsible advocate for his fellow Palestinians.

I salute him for his consistency, his integrity, and his devotion. I am proud to call him my friend.

George P. Shultz was U.S. secretary of state from 1982 to 1989.

Be Frank with the World

Ray R. Irani

H asib Sabbagh's philosophy of life is perhaps best reflected in a quotation from a letter General Robert E. Lee wrote to his son in 1860. Lee wrote:

> You must be frank with the world. Frankness is the child of honesty and courage. Just say what you mean to do on every occasion, and take it for granted you mean to do right. If a friend asks you a favor, you should grant it, if it's reasonable. If not, tell him plainly why you cannot. You will wrong him and wrong yourself by equivocation of any kind. Never do a wrong thing to make a friend or keep one. Above all, do not appear to others what you are not.

As a student at the American University of Beirut (AUB), I often heard about Hasib Sabbagh. He was known as one of the most prominent and successful alumni, having graduated in 1941 with a bachelor's degree in civil engineering. Everybody talked about him—teachers, students, and business and political leaders. In 1943, Hasib founded the Consolidated Contractors Company (CCC) in Haifa. After fleeing Palestine on April 23, 1948, he re-established the firm in 1950 in Lebanon with the late Kamil 'Abd al-Rahman, Said Khoury, and six other business executives from Syria and Lebanon. CCC was then and is now the dominant construction company in the Middle East.

Ray R. Irani is chairman of the board, president, and chief executive officer of the Occidental Petroleum Corporation.

Armand Hammer, former president of Occidental
Petroleum, and Hasib Sabbagh

Although I had heard and read about Hasib, I did not have the privilege of meeting him until I joined Occidental Petroleum in 1984. I met him through two of my associates at Occidental, the late Armand Hammer and Odeh Aburdene, who was at that time a vice president. During my first meeting with Hasib, his daughter Sana accompanied him. She exuded confidence, charm, and a strong intellect. Hasib struck me as a man who knew a great deal, but said little. In subsequent conversations with him, I began to see him as a man of wisdom, experience, fairness, shrewd judgment, vision, infinite generosity, civic commitment to his society and people, and, most importantly, a person who always kept his word.

As I got to know Hasib during the years of 1984 to 1986, it became apparent that he worked hard at making and keeping friends. His attention was always focused on the other person during a conversation. Although strong-willed, I have found that he does not like confrontation but, rather, tends to be conciliatory and thoughtful.

In the process of getting to know Hasib, I learned a profound lesson: Decide what it is you want to do, and then start doing it. This is his basic philosophy. In essence, Hasib is an unstinting teacher. He inspires you with his enthusiasm for your project. He has little patience with phonies, but great patience with people who are sincerely trying to do their best. As General Lee advocated, he is frank with the world and does not appear to others to be what he is not.

Two qualities make Hasib unique as a businessman: an ability to cold-bloodedly dissect opportunities, problems, and personalities, and an iron determination to follow through and get what he wants. Through a shrewd combination of personal relationships—his own and those of colleagues such as Said Khoury—word of mouth, and the leverage afforded his company by association with the Arab Bank and its chairman, Abdul Majid Shoman, Hasib became one of the best connected and most knowledgeable businessmen in the Arab world.

He created one of the finest construction companies in the Middle East. The firm hired the best people it could find, seeking capable, experienced persons who were highly motivated and who wanted to achieve and make something of their lives. CCC made sure that it hired persons who shared an enthusiasm for work. In order to retain such executives and engineers, CCC paid higher salaries and supplemented them with generous bonuses. It also moved personnel up quickly through the ranks. Most importantly, Hasib earned the loyalty of his employees by showing and expressing empathy and sensitivity during times of distress. One quality I have observed in Hasib is rare indeed: he makes it clear to his associates that he wants honest opinions at all times. People may disagree with him, or with anyone else, and no one will suffer as a consequence.

My company's successful involvement in Yemen is due to Hasib's vision, knowledge, and contacts. Hasib's involvement in that country goes back to the period of 1950 to 1952, when he went to Aden and participated in building a refinery with Bechtel-Wimpey. In 1953, Hasib visited Yemen three times with his technical team to study and prepare documents for the San'a-Hodaydah road, later built by the Chinese. Hasib's name in Yemen, and the reputation of CCC, opened doors and lent an aura of permanence and respectability to any project in which they were involved.

Because of Hasib's knowledge of Yemen and his contacts, Occidental decided to seek, through Canadian Oxy Petroleum Limited, of which I am also chairman, a concession in South Yemen in partnership with CCC. (Such opportunities were not open to U.S. oil companies then.) Hasib and CCC assisted Canadian Oxy in its negotiations with the government of

Yemen, and on March 15, 1987, an agreement for petroleum exploration
and production was signed. Without Hasib and CCC, our efforts in Yemen
would not have been successful. Canadian Oxy filed a declaration of commercial discovery on December 18, 1991. In December 1992, Canadian
Oxy filed a second declaration of commercial discovery. On September
26, 1993, commercial production commenced at the rate of 125,000 barrels of oil per day.

After the oil discovery, the consortium led by Canadian Oxy selected
CCC to develop and build a major facility for the export of crude oil. The
Yemen Masila export project was huge and was divided by CCC into nine
major areas, each highly complex and requiring the latest technology: a
gathering system, central production facility, pump station, pipeline, export terminal, offshore facilities, SCADA and communications,
infrastructure, and power generation and distribution.

CCC was selected on the basis of the firm's success in building a pipeline for the Hunt and Exxon oil companies in Yemen. In the late 1960s,
CCC had helped Occidental develop vast oil fields in Libya. It had technical know-how, good relations with local authorities, and, most importantly,
Hasib promised that the job would be done on time, no matter what. Despite the difficult terrain and the remoteness of the oil fields, Hasib
committed CCC to having the export facility operating by September 26,
1993, the National Day of Yemen.

Hasib and CCC did what they said they would do, and when I visited
Yemen in September 1993 for the inauguration of the export facility, all of
Yemen—from the president to tribal chiefs, from oil ministry officials to
people in the street—thanked Occidental, CCC, and Hasib. The Yemeni
people have known Hasib since the 1950s, so after forty years of work in
Yemen, Hasib and his company have amassed goodwill, credibility, and
respect. The people of Yemen look to Hasib and CCC as contributors to
Yemeni national development rather than as exploiters of their resources.
Hasib's success in Yemen shows that he is full of wisdom, big in his ways
of relating to people, and tall in his accomplishments, vision, loyalty, and
generosity.

Since 1970, Hasib has spent nearly half of his time extending his influence on behalf of the Palestinian people and peace in the Middle East.
Indeed, peace in the Middle East is his passion, and he and I have spent

hours discussing his vision and outlook. He has traveled to the United States, Europe, and throughout the Middle East in pursuit of peace. I have seen him meet with presidents, kings, statesmen, diplomats, and journalists to exchange ideas. He has presented his views to Presidents Jimmy Carter and Ronald Reagan. He has sat with and discussed the search for peace with Secretaries of State George Shultz and Warren Christopher. He dines with key leaders and officials in the Untied States, Europe, and the Arab world to promote peace and stability in the Middle East. His commitment to peace is as strong as his commitment to his family, friends, and company. Promoting peace and encouraging and accepting negotiations at every level, Hasib believes, is a rule of wisdom that draws both heavenly and earthly blessings.

By working hard and taking risks in countries that face economic and political difficulties, Hasib and his company have done well financially. Money to him is a tool to be used to express generosity, to cement the ties of family and company, and to press for peace. He never panicked when times were hard. I think it never occurred to him that he could not make more money. After the death of his wife Diana Tamari in 1978, he founded a private philanthropic foundation in her name, and he pays five percent of his income into this fund. Hasib's generosity is global. He has funded universities, hospitals, and charities in Gaza, the West Bank, Jordan, and Lebanon. He has contributed to major universities including Harvard and Georgetown, and he has helped hospitals such as Massachusetts General in Boston and the Cleveland Clinic. His biggest contributions, however, have gone to his alma mater, the American University of Beirut, and to building a major hospital near Jerusalem. He has done this with humility and without fanfare. Hasib Sabbagh figures in history with a capital "H." What is much more important, however, is that he is a human being of great depth, breadth, and remarkable generosity.

Comfortable with Silence

A. Robert Abboud

Hasib Sabbagh is a friend, closer to me than a blood brother—one
that I love and respect—making it virtually impossible for me or
anyone else to describe him factually or dispassionately. The encompass-
ing icon for Hasib Sabbagh to me is source of strength. Father to two
sons—Samir and Suheil—and to his daughter—Sana—he was also the
devoted husband of Diana Tamari, whom he deeply loved. Brother to four
sisters—Suad, Munira, Najla, and Wadad—he is, besides, uncle, cousin,
brother-in-law, friend, counselor, employer, and patriarch. He is chairman
of a most successful worldwide company. Philanthropist without reserva-
tion, he is a pillar of the church. A person of wisdom and vision, he possesses
genuine compassion and is a steady beacon of light to his Palestinian countrymen and women, pointing the way through the decades of their diaspora.
A humanitarian who has known personal tragedy and grief, he empathizes
with people at every level, particularly those who are poor, hurt, homeless,
or helpless. He genuinely revels in the joy, accomplishments, and victories
of others and listens with understanding and feeling, offering wisdom and
advice if solicited, yet remaining silent if not entreated. It is said that Win-
ston Churchill admonished others not to speak unless they could improve
upon the silence. I have always believed it to be significant and revealing
of character that Hasib is comfortable with silence.

To family, friends, neighbors, business associates, educators, scien-
tists, medical practitioners, political leaders, clergymen, and cultural leaders,

---

*A. Robert Abboud, a former Marine Corps captain, has had a long and distin-
guished career as a banker, financier, and head of major American corporations.*

Hasib is a source of strength. In all of these relationships, he has remained unswervingly faithful to his most treasured values: honor, loyalty, and fair play. Live by these values and you will earn Hasib Sabbagh's friendship and respect. Compromise these values or shade them in the slightest and no matter how close your previous relationship, you will lose his friendship and respect. The loss may not be overt, but you will come to know it, without a spoken word or conscious act. On the other hand, if you err and genuinely confess and are sincere in your remorse, you will be forgiven without prejudice or lingering suspicion. He communicates his standards by example and makes all of us better and stronger from our being with him.

Above all, Hasib Sabbagh is a family man and the forum of last resort for all major issues, personal or business. This is a burden of leadership he carries with grace, style, and compassionate understanding. As the head of the family, he has taken great care to provide as fully as possible for succeeding generations both spiritually and tangibly, always accenting age-old family traditions, customs, and pride of heritage. I can attest from personal involvement to his uncompromising and overriding priority of keeping his family together, unified, and symbiotic. This goal is of utmost importance, one on which he spares no expense or effort to make happen, although our modern, global world sometimes seems unsympathetic toward his intent. He has been successful largely through dogged perseverance and commitment.

He laughs at one vignette involving his late beloved sister Suad and the church. One year Hasib took the family to a Christmas service in Rome at which the pope was offering the mass. They were seated in front among throngs of other worshippers and flickering candles. As the mass proceeded Hasib, becoming impatient, beckoned to the family to follow him in slipping out a side aisle before the service was completed. Suad resisted and signaled so, but Hasib eventually prevailed. On the way out, Suad fell and hurt herself because of a slippery spot on the floor. From that day forward, she admonished Hasib that by walking out on the pope he had strayed, with her fall the punishment for his transgression. He tells the story with humor, but deep down I think he may believe it, and I do too.

A more sobering recollection involved Hasib's house in Beirut. When the Israelis invaded in 1982 and pushed northward into this beautiful city,

Hasib was first and foremost concerned with the suffering of the people at large, particularly those in the squalid refugee camps who were enduring the brunt of the assaults. Yet, I recall that he was also concerned about the room in his house that had belonged to his late departed wife, a room that was kept intact in reverence and love for her. That same love extends to his remaining immediate and extended family, without boundary or limit.

Respecting all sincere religion, Hasib fervently believes in the right of each person to practice it in his or her own way. This ecumenical posture is not practiced on political grounds, but is a genuinely cherished value. He supports all religions and the cause of interfaith dialogue. With legions of friends everywhere in the world, he has won their fealty because he genuinely respects people for who they are, while they respect him for his genuineness and sincerity.

If called for help, he does not hesitate, provided the call is appropriate and legitimate. I recall one such occasion in 1979. U.S. special trade negotiator Robert Strauss was instructed by President Jimmy Carter to ask Saudi Arabia to increase its oil production to virtual capacity—10 million barrels a day. Bob telephoned me to see if I would be willing to find out quietly if the request that he proposed to make would be well received. I called Hasib, who used his own goodwill to secure an appointment for him and me with then-Crown Prince Fahd. We met. The crown prince could not have been more gracious. The meeting was a success; I informed Bob Strauss of this, and he pursued his mission to Saudi Arabia, successfully executing President Carter's request.

Paradoxically, Hasib also appreciates that close personal friendship is not always a guarantee of business assistance. When I was president of the Occidental Petroleum Corporation, we needed to build a pipeline in Colombia, South America. Hasib's company, Consolidated Contractors Company (CCC), was interested in being a participant. Strenuous negotiations were conducted with many parties, and the bid was awarded to Mannesman—not the group with which CCC was allied. This was a bitter disappointment to CCC, and to Hasib personally. Yet Hasib has stated publicly on more than one occasion, friendship cannot influence duty or honor; he went one step further and told me that I had made the right decision. This is the badge of a true confidant. As a friend, Hasib is candid, his word his bond. He tells the truth, as he understands it, to royalty, government leaders, and everyday associates alike.

A committed and dedicated patriot for the Palestinian people, Hasib has worked tirelessly to secure self-governance for Palestinians. He has served as a communications link between parties for moderation and reason in efforts to achieve a peaceful resolution of their plight. When his Palestinian countrymen and women were unmercifully attacked in refugee camps as they were in the 1982 Israeli invasion of Beirut, he was relentless in calling anyone and everyone, including me, to implore the U.S. government to intervene to stop the slaughter. Intervention did finally occur, when the U.S. Marines landed.

Although deeply and emotionally committed to the Palestinian cause, I find it most compelling that Hasib has never lost perspective or reason. He has participated actively in conferences and discussions with Arabs, Israelis, and others seeking to find formulae for resolution. He worked closely with Phillip Klutznick, when Phil was head of the Jewish World Congress. He has met with presidents, monarchs, secretaries of state, and foreign ministers. He has sponsored intellectuals and academicians for study in institutions of higher learning and made it possible for some to serve as theoreticians advising the Palestinian government-in-exile. Even today, he is deeply committed to convincing his fellow Palestinians of the need for democratic institutions to be built by the embryonic government in the West Bank and Gaza. He understands the imperative for the creation of institutions and their staffing with capable, competent public servants who can establish the base for urgently needed economic development.

As a humanitarian, Hasib's involvement with and commitment to hospitals, foundations, clinics, universities, and institutions for education and learning needs little elaboration, but what is most striking is that Hasib's humanitarianism is more than merely a generosity to do good. It is benevolence directed at rebuilding the spirit and cultural pride of a devastated people and the human race. Hasib believes in human dignity and the worth of the individual, which, if nurtured, will give rise to creativity and good works, or alternatively, if destroyed or demeaned, will cause despair and misery. Give people dignity is Hasib's conviction; give them health and a sense of well-being, a cultural heritage, self-esteem, and pride. Make these attributes possible, and their own talents for good will flourish and their commitment to peace, a beneficial social structure, and an uplifting faith will prosper.

I worked with Hasib on an innovative project to bring the ancient art and antiquities of Mesopotamia to the United States in cooperation with Washington's leading and most respected cultural institutions—our objective being to preserve and educate through the artifacts of Mesopotamian civilizations, so important to the beginnings of the history of the Western world. It was also testament to the sophisticated arts and sciences that emanated from the peoples of the Tigris–Euphrates Valley, forming the foundation for the succeeding Middle Eastern cultures and societies that ultimately and immeasurably continue to enrich our civilization today. Unfortunately, this project was brought to a halt by the 1990–91 Gulf War.

Hasib Sabbagh's success in business is legendary and well documented. As exiles and refugees from their native Palestine in which their families had lived since time immemorial, he and his brother-in-law Said Khoury and others formed CCC. The early years must have been tumultuous and challenging, yet, by the time my personal involvement with Hasib began, in the late 1960s and early 1970s, I was struck by his quiet strength, vision, ability to extrapolate from current events into future trends, and his ability to lead. Hasib has told me on many occasions of a credo that has meaning for him, one that he attributes to J. Paul Getty: "Put yourself in the other person's shoes and work a solution that benefits both parties. Then pick very able people in whom you have confidence to execute the transaction."

The ability to listen and empathize, to understand and relate to the other person's point of view, is what makes Hasib Sabbagh successful in business. Combined with an unwavering decisiveness, this is the hallmark of any successful business leader, and it is all the more important when conducting business in a part of the world where politics and personal relationships are crucial. Political involvement and acuity are also indispensable ingredients for survival and success; Hasib's sharp insights guide his political involvement and his keen instincts hone his political awareness.

Over the years, Hasib and I have worked on a number of projects together, in the Middle East and elsewhere in the world. In all of these ventures, the quality that impressed me most was Hasib's ability to project his strength and integrity and confidence in his company to prospective clients from the very first moment of their initial meeting. I have seen how he operates time and again. Typically, Hasib enters and remains silent, yet listening intently. At just the right moment he will come forward with a breakthrough insight or cogent comment, capping it off with a commitment, on the spot, for what CCC can or cannot do. His projected confidence and sincerity are always disarming and, because of the chemistry thus established, subsequent negotiations on framework and details become focused and directed toward consummation. Hasib Sabbagh and Said Khoury make a fine team guiding CCC, and their talents and skills complement each other without politics—which is not always the case in most businesses—because it is all in the family.

Logistics were never a hindrance for Hasib. We would go anywhere, under any circumstance, irrespective of comfort or conditions, patiently waiting for hours or days if necessary, always with the objective of achievement. Hasib would never complain of personal pain or discomfort. I remember one occasion, when he was visiting my home in Chicago, on which he had broken his foot. Surely he was in severe pain, yet he would not accept medication, continued his schedule of meetings without interruption, and disguised his anguish to all but the very few of us who knew him well enough to see what he was forcing himself to endure.

At one stage, it became necessary for CCC to look ahead and devise more formalized procedures for corporate governance in anticipation of a future leadership succession. The firm of Hay Associates was hired to consult with CCC regarding its organization and corporate governance, and I had the good fortune to work with the group during part of this period. Anyone who has participated in such an undertaking appreciates how difficult and emotionally draining the process can be, and CCC was no exception to this rule. At last, the objective was achieved. Hasib, as the chairman and sponsor of the project, had his leadership skills taxed to the utmost, yet, once again, his fortitude showed in his comfort with silence and disdain for unnecessary verbiage. Using few words, he deftly guided the company so that it emerged strong and healthy, its future course and direction firmly established.

The Other Refugee

Odeh F. Aburdene

To fathom Hasib Sabbagh's frankness, straightforward gaze, occasional bluntness, and, also, his genius, you must first understand his view of education. His is an outlook on education-for-life that was perhaps best expressed by a professor of moral philosophy at Oxford University early in the century who grumbled, "Nothing that you will learn in the course of your studies will be of the slightest possible use to you in after life—save only this—that if you work hard and diligently you should be able to detect when a *man is talking rot,* and that in my view is the main, if not the sole, purpose of education." It was Professor J. A. Smith who in 1914 said these words, and yet they perfectly anticipated Hasib's idea of what makes for true education, which for Hasib—when combined with spare words and practical wisdom—have made for a formula for success in almost everything he touches.

When I met Hasib in Chicago in 1976, my first impression was of a peerless husband and tender father. As he was accompanied by his late wife Diana and daughter Sana, I could easily see his gentleness and attention toward his wife and the deep pride he took in his children, especially his talented and articulate daughter. Throughout the years of our friendship, this quality has remained one of his most transcendent strengths, and it is all the more notable because so few men are sure-footed enough to show affection publicly. Anyone who knows Hasib well, however, under-

Odeh F. Aburdene is an oil economist by training who is now an investment banker in New York City.

stands that his family comes first and that they are his abiding preoccupation no matter where in the world he may be.

As I came to know him better as a person, I was concurrently becoming aware from other sources that Hasib was one of the Arab world's preeminent businessmen. He never said this of himself, however. He has too much modesty. His firm, Consolidated Contractors Company (CCC), is recognized as the best and most businesslike firm in the Middle East and Africa. Indeed, CCC has come to represent efficiency in a region where the meaning of time is sometimes blurred. How he had done this perplexed and intrigued me. Subsequently, I saw that his achievement was even more significant than I had thought: along with his partner Said Khoury, he had actually created the best corporate organization in the Middle East.

I watched Hasib closeup for many years, hoping to learn from his technique, and I noticed that he imparted enthusiasm, vigor, geniality, self-confidence, decisiveness, and perhaps most of all, an iron discipline among those with whom he interacted. By selecting people on the basis of their intelligence and talent, and then encouraging these attributes, he was able to build on their personal strengths. Perhaps most amazing was that Hasib's management approach had made his subordinates and associates wealthy; an astonishing number of those who have worked for him have become wealthy beyond their dreams. Hundreds of Palestinians have been made millionaires because of him, and what is even more notable and extraordinary, their accomplishments have only served to give him more pride and pleasure. I have concluded that it is his personal character and sure sense of himself that has enhanced his business acumen rather than (as is often the case) his success at business that has built his feelings of self-worth. Virtue sometimes seems to have disappeared as a value in our postmodern age, yet, for Hasib Sabbagh, it is a driving force in much the way Aristotle has written:

> As man is the best of the animals when perfected, so he is the worst when separated from law and justice. For injustice is most dangerous when it is armed, and man, armed by nature with good sense and virtue, may use them for entirely opposite ends. Therefore, when he is without virtue man is the most unscrupulous and savage of animals.

A natural leader, Hasib easily earns the respect of associates and clients. In addition, he has an aptitude for developing deep friendships. Every relationship is to him pivotal and significant, and he has uncannily been able to forge friendships with people of different philosophies, sometimes where there are complex disagreements. He maintains hundreds of relationships worldwide among persons of all faiths and political persuasions, and he is continually expanding his circle of friends. Persons matter more than concepts to Hasib. Relationships are worth more than wealth. Ralph Waldo Emerson once said, "An Institution is the lengthened shadow of a man." CCC is the lengthened shadow of Hasib Sabbagh.

Through his incomparable network of elite contacts in the Arab world and the West, Hasib became an apt "insider," his flair for resolving conflicts through creative compromises manifesting itself in countless interventions that in less competent hands would have only led to friction. Hasib not only knows where decisions are made, he knows many of the people who make them, and he can rely on his well-established network of friends, occupying pivotal positions not only in government but also in business, to ensure that practical solutions are realized.

Hasib always chooses principles over tactics. He despises hypocrisy and has a rage against pomposity and injustice. Yet he also remains in the background as much as possible, shunning the limelight as something painfully to be avoided. One extraordinary example comes to mind: In 1979 Hasib played a critical role in a major regional crisis, and yet it is something about which I have never heard him speak, much less try to take credit. On 4 November 1979, the U.S. embassy in Tehran was occupied by students who were fanatic in their extremism, and sixty-three Americans in the embassy were seized. Within twenty-four hours, the U.S. embassy in Beirut asked Hasib if he could have Yasir Arafat, chairman of the Palestine Liberation Organization (PLO), use his influence in Tehran to free the hostages. In short order, Hasib's house in Beirut became the meeting ground for indirect and informal channels to Iran—and also for unofficial contact between the PLO and the U.S. government—his living room the vortex for three-way contacts between parties who were publicly not in communication with each other. On approximately 9 November, Hasib telephoned me in Chicago and asked to speak with my superior, A. Robert Abboud.

Bob was at that moment traveling in China. Hasib suggested that Bob should fly back to Chicago and ready himself for a trip to Jeddah to meet with then-Crown Prince Fahd. Before going to Jeddah, Hasib advised, Bob should telephone his friend Robert Strauss, the Carter administration's special envoy to the Middle East, in Washington, and talk with him about the hostage issue. He did so. It was Hasib's belief that Fahd was the only person who could sway Chairman Arafat personally to intervene with Ayatollah Ruhollah Khomeini, and to do so with sufficient vehemence and conviction that it would result in the ayatollah's ordering the release of the hostages.

Before we left for Saudi Arabia, Bob Abboud was also in frequent contact with Warren Christopher, who was then undersecretary of state and in charge of the hostage affair. In a matter of days, Bob and I flew to Jeddah with a message from the Carter administration. Hasib met us in Jeddah and took Bob to Fahd's home late at night. As a result, at the end of their meeting, the crown prince telephoned Chairman Arafat in Beirut and asked him to use the full force of his influence in Tehran to get the hostages freed. Fahd told the chairman that the hostage issue was of the utmost importance both to him personally and to Saudi Arabia. Subsequently, in response to Fahd's plea, Arafat sent his top advisor and associate, Khalil Wazir (Abu Jihad), to Tehran to urge Ayatollah Khomeini to release the hostages. On 17 November, Ayatollah Khomeini issued a directive for the deliverance of thirteen female and black hostages. In his book *Hard Choices,* Secretary of State Cyrus Vance documents the PLO's help in obtaining the hostages' freedom.

During the meeting with Crown Prince Fahd, Bob Abboud expressed to the future king the wish of President Carter to see Saudi Arabia increase its oil production to offset the shortfall from Iran's lack of production, and thus to help stabilize world oil prices. The price had gone up to $34 dollars a barrel, and global inflation had risen sharply. U.S. dollar interest rates had hit nearly 19 percent. Fahd responded positively. This was officially confirmed when, ten days later, Robert Strauss called on the crown prince, who conveyed to President Carter's emissary that Saudi Arabia would be increasing production. The decision had a dramatically positive effect on the world economy for, as Saudi production rose over time, U.S. interest

Hasib and Sana Sabbagh being greeted by U.S. vice president George Bush,
Saudi crown prince Fahd, and Saudi prince Bandar in Washington, D.C., 1981

rates began to decline, inflation dropped worldwide, and oil prices began
to retreat. As so often happens, the significance of this venture would have
unanticipated effects: President Ronald Reagan was to be the beneficiary
of this intervention and reap the economic benefits of lower oil prices.
Nonetheless, Hasib Sabbagh was a silent but happy man.

Hasib's generosity is well known and was instilled in him by his mother,
who taught him that if someone asks you for something and you can give
it, then you must give. Hasib practices this philosophy daily. He also goes
one step further and offers help before being asked. Many a person too
diffident or defeated to ask has received help from Hasib. Scholarships
have been written for needy students, and he has paid the medical bills of
persons who cannot afford medical treatment in the United States or Europe. I have watched him respond to the ache of people too shy to inquire,
and give solace to others before they are able to mouth the words of a
request. The marvel is that he sometimes helps people before they have
acknowledged to themselves that they may need assistance. Recently, a
young Palestinian professor teaching in the United States who had devoted his adult life to the Palestinian cause returned to his home in
Jerusalem, where he was diagnosed with cancer. As soon as Hasib heard
this news, he made arrangements for the young man's admission to one of

the world's finest medical centers and sent $30,000 to cover the treatments; sadly, he died an untimely death, but this is one example of many of Hasib's generosity and caring.

On his own, Hasib remembers those who are in despair around holidays and tries to bring joy to lonely, mourning, or sorrowful families, yet what makes this so remarkable is that these feats have no aura of Victorian largesse nor scent of condescending charity. He acts to benefit others with no thought of himself or self-aggrandizement. Thus, no one ever feels patronized by his gifts. The spontaneous, natural, and heartfelt nature of his acts in helping someone else was inculcated in him at so young an age that it is completely and utterly without self-consciousness.

Hasib is almost a father to me, and his encouragement, understanding, confidence, and trust in me have bridged enormous differences in generational outlook, wealth, and position. An essential humility at the heart of his being makes it possible for me to forget that he so outranks me. More importantly, he has been a good mentor, and as the German philosopher Goethe once said, a good mentor is someone who tells you, "If I accept you as you are, I will make you worse . . . if I treat you as though you are what you are capable of becoming, I help you become that." Hasib is such a mentor.

More than a century ago, a prominent Jewish thinker said, "We are everywhere guests and nowhere the hosts." Since 1948, the Palestinians have been dispersed all over the world and find themselves neither guests nor hosts. Most of them, like Hasib Sabbagh, feel that they are permanently refugees, no matter their circumstances. Despite all of Hasib's successes and the plenitude of his accomplishments and possessions, this man of deep roots who possesses such a strong central sense of direction still feels like a wanderer without a homeland. Years ago, Senator Edward M. Kennedy showed that he understood the emptiness that comes from loss of identity. A young Alaskan, a Native American woman named Margaret Nick, was quoted by Senator Kennedy in *Look* magazine on June 2, 1970: "Some people say that a man without education might as well be dead. I say, a man without identity—if a man doesn't know who he is—he might as well be dead." Hasib is the other refugee that we do not hear about. He, and those he has helped, represent the majority of Palestinians who are silent in enduring their constant ache; they do not make headlines, and you will not see them on CNN or the BBC. Having lifted himself, his family, and many other refugees out of the slough of hopelessness and resignation, Hasib has given more of his fortune and, perhaps most importantly, more of his feelings to the Palestinian cause than any other person I know. The struggle for identity as a Palestinian and quest for fulfillment, along with the dream of a Palestinian state that will be democratic, tolerant, and thriving with a market economy—these are the thoughts that fill Hasib's days and nights.

A Builder of Hopes

David Rockefeller

M y first interest and knowledge of the Middle East was ignited in
1929 by a trip on which my parents took me to Egypt, where we
spent several weeks going up the Nile and then on to Palestine. My first
visit to Jerusalem is one that I will never forget. I went back again, while
in the army during World War II, and spent quite a lot of time there. During
the days that I was with the Chase Manhattan Bank, I traveled to the Middle
East a great many times. It was during those trips that I first had the privilege of meeting Hasib Sabbagh, in Lebanon in the early 1970s, and then
we met again at the International Industrial Conference in San Francisco
in 1977.

It was quite clear to me from those early years that Hasib was one of
the outstanding leaders of the Middle East. I have, therefore, been particularly pleased to have had a chance to see him more recently, along with his
lovely daughter Sana, at Harvard, which not surprisingly has recognized
what a remarkable man Hasib is. He has been a great friend and supporter
of Harvard.

For all these reasons I find it especially appropriate that we pay tribute

*David Rockefeller, now honorary chairman of the Council on Foreign Relations,
was its chairman from 1970 to 1985. He was chairman of the Chase Manhattan
Bank from 1969 to 1981, culminating a thirty-five-year career at the bank. He
now chairs the bank's International Advisory Committee. "A Builder of Hopes"
is based on remarks he delivered at the Council on Foreign Relations Board of
Directors Dinner, October 11, 1994, held in honor of Hasib Sabbagh on the occasion of the establishment of the Hasib J. Sabbagh Chair of Middle East Studies.*

to Hasib Sabbagh. Yet, in reality, it is he who honors us by his presence. For it is his exemplary career that reminds us how privileged we are to share this moment with him, his family, and intimate friends, many of whom I have also had the privilege of knowing over the years.

Hasib Sabbagh is not merely a builder of things on a grand scale—those pipelines and bridges and refineries and roads and hospitals that have made Consolidated Contractors Company the most successful construction company in the Middle East. He is also a builder of hopes for the Palestinian people. He has nurtured their well-being as a patron and an employer. He has supported their education, knowing that superior education has been, and will always be, a badge of Palestinian achievement. Like his ancestor Ibrahim Sabbagh, who three centuries ago claimed independence of his people from the Ottoman sultanate, Hasib Sabbagh has believed passionately in the political destiny of his people. They are now more secure, fortunately, and more prosperous, and he has had a big hand in helping to bring about these improvements.

He is a builder of peace and reconciliation in a Middle East that has known precious little coexistence during most of his lifetime. He worked for peace long before it seemed within reach, against odds far less promising than those of today. In ways still largely unknown and unheralded among the public-at-large, he has made a practical difference that exemplifies the best of his generation of Palestinians.

When a man accomplishes so much but claims so little credit, we marvel at his humility. When his generosity reflects such extraordinary civic and social responsibility, we are moved by his selflessness. When he decides not to await a better future for his people but to shape it actively by himself, we admire his vision and commitment. And when he serves his family, his company, his people, and his values so uncompromisingly, we are witness to the real meaning of loyalty.

A Pivotal Role

Richard W. Murphy

Hasib Sabbagh and I first met when I was U.S. ambassador to Saudi Arabia in the early 1980s, but I did not get to know him well until I became assistant secretary of state for Near Eastern and South Asian affairs in 1983. Our meetings over the next five years were usually at his Washington home over breakfast on my way to the State Department. I vividly remember his breakfast table. It provided a feast containing most of the favorite foods of underemployed cardiologists. It would always be laden with plates of bacon, sausages, two kinds of eggs, Arabic bread, olives, toast, pickles, three different jams, and labneh. He is a good trencherman. When we compared notes on weight loss after extended efforts on our respective rigidly controlled diets, he was extremely proud of having managed to drop two pounds. Knowing of my enthusiasm for cigars, Hasib, at the end of our meetings, would often present me with a box with a fine Cuban brand name. I would slip out of his Wyoming Avenue home and onto the streets of Washington feeling mildly criminal, the cigars carefully concealed in their airport, duty-free bag.

We came to know each other at a moment in U.S.–Middle Eastern diplomacy when knowledge of the thinking in the Palestine Liberation Organization (PLO) was essential for the U.S. government, but direct contact between American officials with the organization itself was forbidden. Hasib, a longtime member of the Palestine National Council (PNC), the organization that the PLO then described as its "supreme legislative body," was a remarkably well-informed commentator. Fortunately, Secretary of

---

Richard W. Murphy is a former assistant secretary of state.

State George Shultz had wisely decided that PNC membership per se did not disqualify U.S. officials from meeting its members. Otherwise, we would have denied ourselves contact with a wide range of prominent Palestinians, including some with U.S. citizenship.

Unquestionably, I derived the greater benefit from our meetings. Hasib would tactfully start our exchange with a general question. He never pressed for detailed information about the state of U.S. thinking concerning the Arab–Israeli peace process. He knew that there might have been developments or projections too sensitive for me to share with those outside our government. Rather, he welcomed a general briefing and would, in turn, share his views about the reasoning in the PLO's leadership circles. I, in turn, shared his insights with Secretary Shultz. For many years, and by all accounts, Hasib spoke frankly to PLO chairman Yasir Arafat, yet was never intimidated by him. Hasib's financial weight may have opened doors to him in the PLO leadership, but I believe it was his clearly selfless desire to help the Palestinian people attain a better life that commended him to all.

December 1988 was a milestone in U.S. diplomatic efforts concerning the Palestinian issue, and a moment in which Hasib played a key role. Chairman Arafat had traveled to Geneva that month to address a special session of the United Nations General Assembly, because Washington had refused him a visa to come to New York. Several sources—including the then-foreign minister of Denmark—had ensured us that Arafat, in his speech to the special session, would, after years of refusing to do so, formally and unequivocally recognize Israel's "right to exist" and would announce his acceptance of UN Security Council Resolutions 242 and 338. This would fulfill the requirements first articulated by Secretary of State Henry Kissinger in 1975 for opening the door to a U.S. government dialogue with the PLO.

To our general surprise, Arafat's much touted speech failed to make his position absolutely clear. His references to Israel's right to exist and the specific UN resolutions were too opaque for the United States to accept. Arafat's advisors reportedly then urged him to make another statement in the context of a press conference planned for the following day. Early that morning, Hasib telephoned me from Geneva to confirm that Washington remained ready to open the dialogue if Arafat explicitly met our conditions. I said that we were constant in our position, but there could be no room for any ambiguity in Arafat's statement. Hasib, I subsequently learned, was either with Arafat in the same hotel room while we were talking or nearby and quickly able to relay the message. I also learned later that Hasib had been under the impression that Arafat was going to make his position clear in his statement the previous day and had been deeply upset with the chairman for not having done so.

I had several exchanges with Hasib during the course of that day. In the end, the chairman, after grumpily noting he was being asked to do a "striptease," made a statement that directly quoted from Security Council Resolution 242 on Israel's "right to exist" and, finally, clearly accepted the two Security Council resolutions in question. The United States opened an official dialogue with the PLO, in Tunis, forty-eight hours later.

Hasib maintained his customary calm throughout our conversations that turbulent day. He knew why I was being so insistent on the need for precision, and realized that the burden for clarity was on Chairman Arafat. He played a pivotal role in helping to persuade the chairman. (The dialogue that started in December continued for the next eighteen months in Tunis. It proved to be frustrating for the PLO because the U.S. side kept the focus so tightly on the issue of terrorism. It was broken off in June 1990, when Chairman Arafat failed to issue a rapid and unequivocal condemnation of an attack attempted by the PLO's Abu Abbas faction on Israeli beaches.)

I stayed in touch with Hasib after I left government service. I was asked to help raise urgently needed funds for a hospital in Gaza that was supported by the Anglican Church. My contacts in the governments of the Arabian Peninsula advised that they would be unable to help because they were obliged by their agreements with Arafat to assist the West Bank and Gaza only through the PLO; they could not earmark their assistance for only one project. I felt that I had no solid prospects for getting assistance other than from the Gulf and, after several weeks, was at the point of concluding that I had reached a dead end. I asked Hasib what to do, and he suggested that I raise the matter with Arafat. I did so, and the chairman told me that he was unable to fund all the deserving projects in the occupied territories. He said, however, that he had absolutely no problem with any independent financing I could arrange and that it need not be channeled through him. Hasib had given me sound practical direction.

Hasib is a man of many fine deeds but notably few words. When his daughter Sana decided to contribute to the funding of a chair at the Council on Foreign Relations to be named in honor of her father, we laid plans for an elaborate testimonial dinner to take place in October 1994. The centerpiece was to be Hasib's own comments. At the dinner, several prominent speakers lauded Hasib's vision and work, reaching variable levels of eloquence. At the appointed moment, Hasib rose slowly (and with evident reluctance) to acknowledge the tributes. As I had cautioned those planning the program, his "major" speech was swiftly over.

As President Jimmy Carter has written in the introduction to this book, Hasib Sabbagh has risen above enmity and bitterness. He has lived through times when those emotions have consumed many Palestinians, and for that matter many Israelis as well. He has soldiered on, building a fine business and family. He has dedicated his public service and his generous personal contributions to helping build a better life for his own people, a life which he sees will only be secured through the achievement of an enduring Middle Eastern peace. This is why all of us have written of him with deep and affectionate respect.